SO-AAC-695

BANTAM BOOKS

TORONTO ● NEW YORK ● LONDON ● SYDNEY ● AUCKLAND

GADGET WARFARE

by

F. Clifton Berry, Jr.

THE PEOPLE SNIFFER

An Air Cavalry trooper points the nozzle of a "People Sniffer" attached to his M-16 rifle. Officially designated as the Manpack Personnel Detector-Chemical, the People Sniffer was supposed to be able to detect the presence of a person from the ammonia present in their perspiration. In practice, the sniffer was too sensitive and the electrochemical device picked up ammonia from other sources including animal dung.

OPERATION PINK ROSE

Incendiary bombs explode on an area of defoliated jungle during Operation Pink Rose. The operation was a test program in which a target area was sprayed twice with defoliant and then once with a drying agent. Then ten flights of three B-52 bombers dropped M-35 cluster incendiary bombers, 42 from each aircraft, into the target area to set fire to it, destroying all vegetation and any concealed enemy bunkers.

THE EXPLODING CLOUD

A large manmade cloud of gaseous explosive erupts over a section of jungle as a fuel air explosive (FAE) is detonated. FAEs were dropped in clusters like conventional bombs and discharged their fuel in droplet form at a preset altitude, usually 1,000 feet. When the cloud exploded, it burnt up all the oxygen present, choking its victims, and the overblast pressure created a shock wave that destroyed everything in its wake.

THE MUTTERING DEATH

Miniguns from an AC-47 Dragon-ship, a fixed-wing gunship, fire into the night at a target on the ground. When all three of its 7.62mm guns fired simultaneously the gunship was capable of delivering 18,000 rounds per minute on an enemy target.

BOMBLIFT

A CH-54 Sky Crane proceeds towards a target area with a 10,000-pound bomb slung beneath it. The Sky Crane was originally used in Vietnam as a workhorse, airlifting heavy equipment in and out of the battle zone and retrieving damaged planes and vehicles. It earned its combat spurs as the only aircraft capable of airlifting a 10,000-pound Daisy Cutter bomb and then dropping it precisely on target to create a jungle clearing in one blast.

EDITOR IN CHIEF: Ian Ballantine.
SERIES EDITORS: Richard Grant, Richard Ballantine.
MAPS: Peter Williams. STUDIO: Kim Williams.
PRODUCED BY: The Up & Coming Publishing Company, Bearsville, New York.

GADGET WARFARE
THE ILLUSTRATED HISTORY OF THE VIETNAM WAR
A Bantam Book/ August 1988

ACKNOWLEDGMENTS
*The ever helpful professional historians at the Army's Center for Military
History and the Air Force's Office of History made preparation of this
volume much easier. I am grateful to them, and to the photo researchers at
the DoD Still Media Depository, for their unfailing assistance.*

LIBRARY OF CONGRESS
Library of Congress Cataloging-in-Publication Data

Berry, F. Clifton.
    Gadget warfare / by F. Clifton Berry, Jr.
        p. cm — (The Illustrated history of the Vietnam War)
    ISBN 0-553-34547-8
        1. Vietnamese Conflict, 1961-1975—Technology.   I. Title.
    II. Series.
    DS559.8.S3B37 1988
    959.704'38—dc19   88-8612
                                                                        CIP

Published simultaneously in the United States and Canada

PRINTED IN THE UNITED STATES OF AMERICA

CW 0 9 8 7 6 5 4 3 2 1

Contents

Faith in technology

The quest for the ultimate weapon

"IF YOU COULD have the ultimate weapon delivered tomorrow morning, what would it be?" Working out an answer to the question took us an hour. After heated discussion, we finally came up with a weapon we could all agree upon.

We were watching the sun set over the dark-green jungled hills of the Annamite chain. The day had been a hot, dusty, frustrating one. Most days were like that in the Vietnam War. This one had the usual share of frustrations, uncertainties, ambiguities, and hazards.

It was the autumn of 1967. Our four infantry battalions of the US Army's 196th Light Infantry Brigade were operating around Chu Lai in the provinces of Quang Ngai and Quang Tin.

Four large groups of people uneasily coexisted in the region. They were the US forces; the forces of South Vietnam (ARVN); the people who lived in the area; and the enemy, the Viet Cong (VC) and North Vietnamese Army (NVA) troops. Each group had different goals.

The VC and NVA troops were trying to kill us. They were doing a fair job of it. But we were striking back, killing and wounding the VC and NVA when we found them, and attempting to keep them away from the Chu Lai air base and the population. The ARVN units at that time tended to be held in their cantonments while their army built up its strength. As for the people, some of them supported the VC and some leaned toward the government in Saigon. Most simply wanted to be left alone.

The discussion of the ultimate weapon focused on our own situation. An infallible mine detector was clearly needed. So was a device to see through darkness and fog. A lightweight bulletproof garment

Stay cool —Material innovations was the name the Army gave to much of the gadgetry it developed during the Vietnam War. But the traffic was not all from the top down. Here a guard occupies a classic example of grunt-level innovation as he stays cool, comfortable, and shaded from the sun in his armchair observation post built from discarded ammunition boxes.

would be great. A cloak that made you invisible would suit nicely. Someone wanted a time machine, another wanted a way to stop the oncoming monsoon rains.

All of those sounded great. But we finally settled on what would be the ultimate weapon for us for the time and place: a Truth Detector Ray. Point it at someone, and ask whether they were on our side or the enemy's. The TD Ray would say which, absolute certainty guaranteed. With that certain knowledge, we could separate the bad guys from the good guys and win the war.

The conversation was an indulgence in fantasy. We wanted gadgets to solve our problems. Somehow the miraculous gadgets would eliminate ambiguities and frustrations, and let us go home.

The nighttime fantasizing soon passed. The Truth Detector Ray never materialized. You never could tell by looking whether a Vietnamese civilian supported the Saigon government or the Viet Cong. Nights were as dark as always, and the monsoon rains came on schedule. But we got gadgets—by the score. As the war progressed, the flow of gadgets turned into a flood.

In Washington and Saigon, and in countless laboratories, the search for gadgets was pressed hard during the Vietnam War years. To many in high levels in Washington, faith in gadgets and numbers replaced reality. By concentrating on gadgets they overlooked or ignored the need to face fundamental truths about fighting a strange war in a far-off place where the old rules did not apply and the old machines were ineffectual.

ARPA, the Advanced Research Projects Agency, was the Defense Department's (DoD) shop for overseeing the most advanced and esoteric developments. Under Secretary McNamara, ARPA sponsored scientific studies and research projects on counterinsurgency techniques and equipment.

ARPA gave the code name of Project Agile to the program for developing new weapons for the US forces in Vietnam, and DoD assigned the Army the responsibility of administering it in Southeast Asia. To run the program, the Army set up a field agency called ACTIV (Army Concept Team in Vietnam). ACTIV coordinated requirements and field testing with two main groupings. First, with the advisers

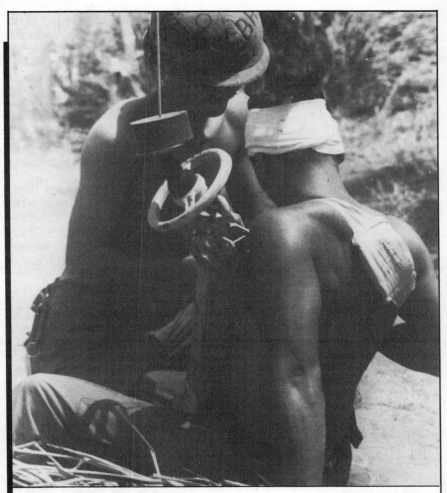

THE PENETRATOR

MEN INJURED or wounded in Vietnam had the comfort of knowing that every effort was being made to evacuate them promptly by helicopter. This knowledge itself served as a great morale-builder and life-saver. Evacuation was usually by a medevac helicopter, known as a Dustoff. But the jungle or the tactical situation often meant that a Dustoff helicopter could not land to pick up a casualty.

To overcome that hazard, the Jungle Penetrator (JP) was developed. A heavy metal probe with a folding saddle, it was lowered through the jungle canopy on a cable paid out by a winch on a hovering Dustoff helicopter. When the JP reached the ground, the troops unfolded the arms of the saddle. The casualty either sat or stood on the arms, or was strapped tight to the JP. A crewman on the helicopter reeled him in.

on the ground, who knew best what the requirements should be. Then, with the depots and manufacturers back in the USA who devised gadgets to meet the requirements.

Other groups and programs with equally anonymous names, which concealed their real purpose, created concepts and developed gadgets during the war. The Jason study group, among other congregations of scientists and academics, developed the concept for the McNamara Line. It was to be the electronic fence that would cut off infiltration and supplies from North Vietnam into the south. The Air Force had its Tactical Air Warfare Center at Eglin Air Force Base (AFB), Florida, which proved to be a fertile proving ground for new ways to fight the war better. At Coronado, California, the Navy concentrated productive efforts to improve its contribution to the war. In Washington, the secretive Defense Communications Planning Group concentrated on developing unmanned sensors that could detect an approaching enemy.

In these and countless other locations, the armed services spent time and money on urgent development of gadgets to meet the peculiar needs of US forces engaged in a peculiar war.

The effort to create these weapons was characteristically American. In Washington, in the defense establishment, and among defense contractors, faith in technology was the new religion. The belief was widespread that American ingenuity could solve any problem, anywhere, anytime. This was the era of the space program, of Saturn rockets and moon landers yearly coming closer to the seemingly impossible dream of putting an American on the moon. To a nation making stunning technological breakthroughs in order to send a series of manned spacecraft on 500,000-mile round-trips to the moon, the technical challenges of the Vietnam War were comparatively minor.

Until Vietnam we had come to think of gadgets as any small, ingenious device or dodge for making an existing task easier. Some of the gadgets that arrived in Vietnam were tiny, like the micro-gravel mines. But others were huge enterprises, such as the massive spraying of herbicides and defoliants on thousands of acres of land.

Most worked. Some did not.

Instant runway —These MN-19 steel runway panels interlocked to provide an immediate hard surface for an airstrip, ramp, or taxiway. Other methods used in Vietnam to create instant airstrips included laying a heavy rubber membrane and spraying chemicals to bind soil particles together.

ENEMY INNOVATION: Without access to much of 20th century technology, the Viet Cong relied on crude but inventive devices to combat US and ARVN forces. These wooden poles, 12-15 feet high, had been placed by the Viet Cong in a rice paddy to prevent helicopter landings.

Whatever their purpose, many of the gadgets developed during the Vietnam War stimulated technological improvements that continue today.

Darkness into light

Modifying climate and weather

IN THE BEGINNING, reports the Book of Genesis, the earth "was without form, and void; and darkness was upon the face of the deep." God soon changed that, creating daylight where before was only darkness.

In Vietnam, the US forces could not split the darkness and turn it into daylight. But they could try to make light in the darkness for a short time at a given place.

Combat infantrymen understood that phrase from Genesis every time night fell in Vietnam. Darkness could be an ally of a well-trained soldier. Under cover of darkness, he could set up outposts for early warning and ambushes to kill enemy troops moving about.

But to the greenseed infantryman spending his first night in a perimeter foxhole, the all-encompassing darkness that shrouded the jungle was a source of fear, the unknown in which the enemy lurked. The almost total absence of twilight in the tropics that saw day become night in a matter of minutes only helped feed his sense of fear. He had only to be in-country a few days to hear the well-worn but often true saying that "the night belongs to Charlie." Charlie came from Victor Charlie, the call sign for the Viet Cong. The expression came from the grunts; it was their half-grudging, half-respectful way of acknowledging that nighttime was when the enemy was at its most active.

And it was true. Darkness served the Viet Cong and North Vietnamese Army as an ally. They moved units and shifted supplies at night. Most attacks on Allied positions were made at night. Attack troops and supporting mortars and rockets moved close during the early hours of darkness, attacked, and

23

Shine up —Troopers of searchlight Battery B, 29th Artillery prepare their Xenon searchlight for the night to come. Extinguishing the Xenon's powerful focusable beam was often a first objective for enemy sappers during attacks on US fire bases.

then disengaged to slip away before daylight came.

Stripping away the protective shade of darkness and denying Charlie the night became a primary goal of the US gadget warfare effort in Vietnam. Success was achieved in several ways.

Flares and searchlights were the crude tools used in earlier wars of the 20th century to convert night into day. In both world wars high-powered searchlights picked out enemy bombers, reaching upwards and pinning them like moths in their beams. Flare shells were common items in the ammo piles stacked behind howitzers and mortars. And hand-held flares were used on outposts and defensive trenches to give early warning.

Effective as they were, these methods had serious limitations. Since flares burned out quickly, scores of them had to be fired in a continuous sequence in order to maintain constant light over an area of the battlefield. Searchlights lasted longer but they also burned out. And neither flares nor searchlights could pierce cloud cover.

But their greatest drawback was that they were, in tactical terminology, "active." They advertised to the enemy that someone was alert, and pinpointed that person's position. The enemy could take action to evade the light or try to put it out.

This did not rule out their use in Vietnam. High intensity flares and lights were used effectively in countless ways. But the drawbacks led to searches for illuminating gadgets that were "passive"; that stripped away darkness and illuminated the enemy without his knowing about it.

One of the earliest passive devices was a direct replacement for the active helicopter-mounted lighting systems used to illuminate ground targets. Known as Firefly and Lightning Bug, they were fitted to UH-1 "Huey" helicopter gunships. A typical arrangement was a fixed bank of landing lights, often cannibalized from a C-123 or C-130 transport aircraft, and fitted in a circular cluster on the open side door of a UH-1 helicopter.

When the helicopter scouting at night found a target, it shone the lights on the target. That bright light made an irresistible target for armed VC, who often opened fire on it. This usually proved to be a mistake, because other gunships followed the lightship. While the lightship illuminated the

Darkness into light

NIGHT LIGHTS:
Two banks of high-intensity arc lamps mounted under the belly of a USAF C-123 transport converted into a lightship. Flying at 12,000 feet over an area under attack, the lamps were capable of providing constant light over an area 2 miles in diameter.

Darkness into light

LIGHTNING BUG:
A UH-1D gunship of an air cavalry unit rigged out for night operations. The cluster of seven landing lights taken from a C-130 transport provided constant bright lighting for night missions. The Huey's main armament was an M-2 machine gun plus 7.62mm miniguns and 2.75-inch rockets.

target, gunships fired into it with their miniguns and rockets.

Refinements and improvements soon followed. When the Cobra gunship arrived, Hueys were freed for a modification called Nighthawk. Nighthawk Hueys were fitted out with a passive night observation device (AN/TVS-4), a Xenon searchlight (AN/VSS-3), and a 7.62mm minigun system (XM-27E1). The searchlight provided intense white light or, if desired, infrared light invisible to the naked eye.

Nighthawk lightships scouted by flying about 500 feet above the ground at 50 knots airspeed. A pair

of Cobra gunships followed, remaining behind and about 1,000 feet above the lightship. From the searchlight, infrared light was shone onto the terrain ahead. The operator could shoot a narrow beam to a range of 2 kilometers, or diffuse the energy over a wider beam to a shorter range.

An observer looking through a hand-held AN/TVS-4 night observation device, a cylindrical 12-inch-long light-gathering scope, saw the scene as illuminated by the infrared light. He scanned the terrain for enemy activity or targets. Unless the enemy had infrared goggles (and they usually did not), the infrared light was invisible.

Maj. Gen. Ellis W. Williamson —the innovative commander of the 25th Infantry Division.

To make the operator's task easier the TVS-4 was mounted coaxially—when the searchlight moved, the scope moved with it. When the observer discovered a target, he switched on the searchlight's white light and directed it smack onto the target or opened fire with the minigun. At that, the gunships swooped in to fire into the target area. Enemy troops quickly learned not to fire at low-flying helicopters and to stay hidden when helicopter noises were heard.

But the most productive use of the Nighthawk helicopters was in response to unmanned sensors that could hear, see, or measure the footfalls of enemy soldiers on the move. One of the driving forces behind developing the Nighthawk for this use was Major General Ellis W. Williamson, who commanded the 25th Infantry Division in 1968-69. He had units of the division place sensor fields in likely places, then await enemy activity. This was in Tay Ninh province, near the Cambodian border.

VC or NVA troops moving at night would trigger unattended sensors. The parent unit would alert the Nighthawk teams, who approached the area using infrared searchlight and the TVS-4 night observation device. A high rate of success attended this technique because of the element of surprise. General Williamson told a Senate committee that in a single month, 103 NVA soldiers were killed by Nighthawks following up sensor indications, without the loss of a single US soldier. Apart from interfering with the Viet Cong's nighttime activities the Nighthawk helicopter and gunship combinations were devastatingly effective in coming to the relief of outposts under attack at night.

THE STARLIGHT SCOPE was the name given to a family of devices that gave US troops the advantage of enhanced night vision. The smallest of the starlight scopes was the AN/PVS-2. It weighed 6 pounds and could be mounted on an M-16 rifle or M-60 machine gun.

On a clear, moonless night, human night vision accommodates to the dark in about 30 minutes. The pupils of the eye dilate, admitting more of the available light. The retina, the responsive layer of specialized nerve cells at the back of the eye, processes the faint light to provide a picture for the

brain to interpret. On outpost duty, an alert, trained soldier could discern movement over a range of about 50 meters.

Using mechanical means, the starlight scope collected even the faintest available light over a 300-meter range and enhanced it many thousands of times. The result was an astonishing conversion of night into day. Viewing through a starlight scope, a gunner scanning a dark landscape suddenly saw it transformed into a clear picture.

Some mental adaptation was required on his part. The scene he saw through the scope did not appear in black and white or colors. Rather, he saw gradations of green and black. But he could "see" clearly, thanks to the manifold enhancement of light.

The light-gathering ability of each model of the starlight scope on issue determined its range. This, in turn, varied according to the amount of moonlight available. The range was shortest when the only illumination came from the stars. On the medium-size starlight scope, which weighed 34 pounds and rested on a tripod, the range was 1,200 meters when the only source of light was the stars.

TWINKLE, TWINKLE: A starlight scope operator squints into a PVS-2A Night Vision Sight Subassembly. The scope gathered low-level ambient light, intensifying it into a coherent picture of the scene not visible to bare eyes. "Twinkle" was a common nickname for scope operators.

NO HIDING PLACE

A Forward Air Controller, riding on the starboard side of an 0-2B Skymaster, uses a hand-held AN/PVS-2A starlight scope. The light-intensifying device proved to be an especially effective tool for Air Force units hunting the enemy along the Ho Chi Minh Trail. A survey comparing two 3-day periods in 1966, before the introduction of the starlight scope, and a similar period in 1967, using the scope, showed the benefits of the device.

TRUCKS SIGHTED	1966	1967
Visually	20	30
Starlight scope	—	597
Destroyed	8	83

Apart from having a range up to 24 times greater than the human eye, the starlight scope was passive. It emitted no sound or rays. The enemy received no clues, no warning that they were being scanned by a GI with a starlight scope mounted on a death-dealing weapon.

But starlight scopes had their limitations. They were fine for close-in viewing on clear, dry nights. But their technology was frustrated by fog, rain, or smoke. And in Vietnam there was plenty of all three.

Instead, when the weather filled in, radar filled the gap. Prior to the Vietnam War radar had seldom been used over short ranges by ground combat troops. The traditional uses of radar were for artillery target acquisition, using radars with ranges up to 20 miles, and in air traffic control and early warning centers where radar sets were effective over hundreds of miles. These sets were either very heavy and bulky, or very expensive, or both. They were unsuitable for close-in tactical purposes.

Two small tactical radar sets had been in the development process for years. Accelerated in development, they were issued to combat battalions early in 1967. The smaller of the two, issued to infantry rifle companies, was the AN/PPS-4 radar, capable of detecting people over a range of 1.5 kilometers (approximately a mile). Positioned on likely enemy approach routes PPS-4 sets responded to indications of movements along a trail by emitting a series of high-pitched tones. Operators required training and practice to discriminate among the tones, but soon mastered the art of being able to tell the sex and size of a person and their position by the sound picture they created.

Battalions were equipped with AN/PPS-5 radar with a range of 5 kilometers (approximately 3 miles). The PPS-5's output was both aural and visual, with the operator listening through headphones and watching a display screen that together provided information on the movement, bearing, and range of the target.

Operators of the PPS-5 and PPS-4 radar sets quickly learned to sort out targets. Crude as the "beeps" were, skilled operators could tell if the target was a man or a woman, and whether they were walking or running, and in which direction. The tone created by a woman walking was a fuzzy *swish, swish* as the radar picked up an alternating return from the way her hips swung. For a man, who created less body movement as he walked, the sound was more distinct. If either broke into a run, the radar emitted a high-pitched *pip, pip, pip*. Because of the Doppler effect, the frequency tone was lower the further the person moved away from the radar, becoming higher-pitched as they came closer.

A KEY CONTACT between the military high command and the scientific community was General

Sound detector —A TPS-33A radar set capable of being broken down into manpack loads for carrying into the combat zone. The TPS-33A could detect people and vehicles on the move at ranges between 100 and 1,800 meters. When a target was detected it generated tones that were audible through earphones and a visual display on a scope.

Westmoreland's scientific adviser, Dr. William G. McMillan, a chemical physicist on leave from UCLA. Westmoreland praised Dr. McMillan for being "at the same time theoretical and pragmatic." The general, commander-in-chief of the US forces in Vietnam from 1964 to 1968, included the scientist in his Saturday morning strategy conferences, hoping to gain a fresh perspective on the military matters under consideration.

Dr. McMillan was listened to with respect. He had correctly forecast the North Vietnamese use of hand-held SA-7 heat-seeking antiaircraft missiles. He was involved in a project to use the weather to impede movement of enemy vehicles on remote mountain roads.

Darkness into light

LISTEN GOOD:
Operators from a ground surveillance squad, 2d Battalion, 16th Infantry, set up AN/PPS-4 radar. Small and portable, the PPS-4 could detect moving targets up to 1,500 meters. A skilled operator could quickly learn to detect the difference between the sound generated by a man and a woman and whether a person was running or walking.

Westmoreland would later recount how Dr. McMillan and his scientists discovered a chemical solvent with ingenious promise. When mixed with water and soil, the solvent turned the soil into slush that would not stabilize so long as it remained wet. They reasoned that unpaved roads used by the enemy as supply routes would be suitable targets for a trial. The hope was that in the rainy season the dirt roads could be turned into quagmires with the stuff.

As Westmoreland told the story, "At the start of the rainy season, they dumped tons of the solvent from C-130s on a constricted road in the war-torn A Shau Valley." But it did not work as tried. Westmoreland said, "no substantial evidence was

33

SMELLING THE LIGHT

TIARA was the name of a light-emitting chemical device that showed promise in laboratory tests. TIARA was inert when kept inside a sealed container. When exposed to the atmosphere, it was chemiluminescent, emitting a light that looked very much like that of fireflies. Possibly it could fill artillery shells, and be fired over an area requiring light. Or, in another application, TIARA mixed with petroleum wax could be kept in a tube like lip balm. Smeared on equipment it gave off a cold light that lasted for up to an hour.

TIARA was first field-tested at the airborne department of the Infantry School at Fort Benning and the Air Force's test center at Eglin AFB. Paratroopers smeared it on the anchor line cables and doors of jump aircraft, making night drops easier. In large quantities it was smeared on signaling panels to mark drop zones.

TIARA tests were held only at night. Only those with high-level security clearance were allowed to handle it. In due course a batch of the chemical was sent to Vietnam for field tests.

The substance that had shown such promise in cool, dry weather proved unreliable in the hot, humid conditions of Vietnam. Its illumination properties were limited; TIARA was all right for marking an object, but inadequate for illuminating an area. But worst of all, it stank. Not a quick, unpleasant smell but a putrid odor that clung to hands and clothing. TIARA went back on the shelf, one of the many gadgets of the Vietnam era that failed to live up to its original promise.

ever found that it proved effective in deterring movement."

Early in the US involvement in Vietnam, several rain-making experiments were tried by seeding clouds from airplanes with silver iodide crystals. The theory was that bad weather would hamper the enemy's movements. But like earlier experiments in the continental US, the cloud-seeding attempts proved futile. General Westmoreland would later report drily that "there seemed to be no appreciable increase in rain." Other highly classified ventures into weather micro-modification were attempted. But even two decades later, the records remain sealed from public inspection.

THE MAIN OBSTACLE in the counterinsurgency war in the thousands of square miles of the Mekong Delta was water. To the Viet Cong the Delta was both a vital transportation artery and a hideaway. Its different cadres exploited to the full the Mekong's countless natural ribbons and the manmade canals that made up a 3,500-mile network.

When it became apparent that American forces would have to take the fight to the enemy in the Delta, ingenuity and improvisation became the order of the day. Both the US Army's 9th Infantry Division and Navy units, which constituted the Mobile Riverine Force, adapted their resources and methods for the brown water war in the Delta region.

While the men of the Mobile Riverine Force may not have been given the ability to walk on water, they certainly came close. Two of the most successful craft adapted for soldiers moving over the water and swamps of the Delta were the Hovercraft and the airboat.

The Hovercraft is a device that moves over any surface on a bubble of air of its own making. The Navy name for its version in the Delta was the Patrol Air Cushion Vehicle, or PACV. It was modified from a Bell Aerosystems commercial craft, 39 feet long and 16 feet high.

The low-pressure bubble of compressed air that lifted the vehicle off the water, so that it could skim almost frictionless and unimpeded over any surface, was generated by a centrifugal lift fan. Forward propulsion was provided by a 9-foot propeller. The PACV's top speed was a phenomenal 75 knots—double that of a conventional warboat.

Although operated by a three-man Navy crew, many considered the PACV to be half-helicopter, half-boat. The bubble of air that was crucial to its operation was contained underneath the vehicle by a flexible canvas skirt. So long as the bubble supported it, the PACV could ignore terrain that would stop other boats or land vehicles, clear solid obstacles up to 3½ feet high, and climb over sloping rice paddy dikes up to 6 feet high. Since nowhere in the Delta is more than 10 feet above sea level, very few obstacles blocked the PACVs.

Hovercraft technology was comparatively new, developed in the late fifties, but only put into commercial use in the sixties. But it was quickly harnessed by the US Navy, which provided its total force of PACVs to support ARVN operations in the Delta during the monsoon of 1966-67. Working with Special Forces airboats and motorized sampans, the PACVs were invaluable in creating havoc among the VC units in the region. But the price was high.

The Mekong Delta —Fertile, heavily populated and riddled with canals and waterways, it provided the Viet Cong with numerous hideaways, ambush points, and escape routes.

Each PACV cost close to $1 million—about the cost of purchasing a small armada of inshore patrol boats. The PACVs were also difficult and costly to service. Technical expertise was in short supply and a PACV could be out of service for several months.

Nonetheless the PACV came through combat tests run by the 9th Infantry Division in January 1968 with satisfactory results. During the trial period each PACV carried from 10 to 12 men and armaments that included M-60 and .50 caliber machine guns, plus a high velocity launcher for 40mm grenades.

The 9th Infantry tested the PACV in 20 offensive operations, skimming unhindered over land, swamps, rivers, and the South China Sea, swooping

Darkness into light

FLOATING ON AIR:
A Patrol Air Cushion Vehicle (PACV) sweeps under the bridge at An Lo in 1966 followed by a second PACV. Half boat, half helicopter, the PACVs were expensive to buy, costing $1 million, noisy to operate and required special maintenance. But they could move faster than ordinary boats and skim over marshes, water, and flat terrain at high speeds in pursuit of the enemy.

into enemy areas at speeds up to 70 knots. When contact was made, the troops piled off the PACV to engage the enemy or capture him. Enemy casualties inflicted in these operations were 43 VC killed and 100 detained. Official US losses were just two wounded soldiers aboard the PACVs.

After the tests, commanders of 9th Infantry Division units requested more PACVs and got them. Cavalry platoons, never slow to make use of the latest equipment, requested and received PACVs for reconnaissance and quick reaction operations, as well as in security missions.

A smaller and considerably less expensive solution to the problem of mobility in the Delta was the use of airboats, introduced by Special Forces advisers.

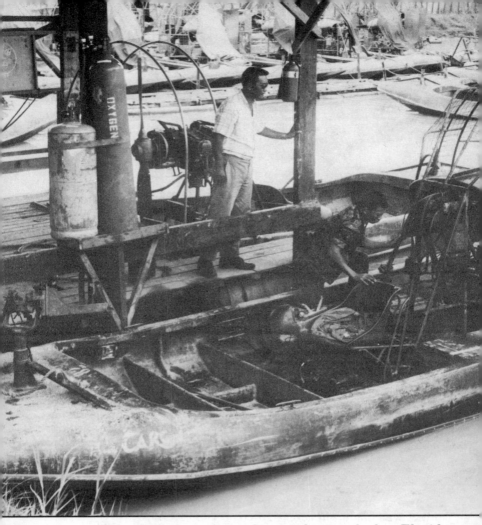

Airboats were the products of the Florida Everglades, shallow draft craft, drawing only a couple of inches of water, and capable of a top speed of 41 knots while carrying a crew of two and up to five soldiers with equipment.

At their peak strength, detachments of the 5th Special Forces in the Delta, the ARVN's IV Corps region, operated some 400 watercraft including 84 airboats. The buildup of US troops in the Delta quickly led to the need for a central base. With no suitable land base available, a decision was made in January 1967 to base the 9th Infantry Division on a manmade island. It was constructed in less than

Darkness into light

WATER SKIMMERS:
These one-man airboats used by the Special Forces were the military equivalent of the airboats popular in the Florida Everglades. They had a shallow draft and were powered by a large rear-mounted propeller that acted like a giant fan. INSET: An operator checks his airboat's swivel-mounted .30 caliber machine gun.

11 months at a major waterway intersection called Dong Tam, a Vietnamese phrase chosen by General Westmoreland. In English, it meant "united hearts and minds."

By dredging sand from the Bassac River and pumping it into what had been rice paddies, an island base covering an area of more than 600 acres was built high enough to stay dry even in the monsoon floods that drenched the region from April to November. The base at Dong Tam used more than 8 million cubic meters of sand to create a brigade-size base camp, hospital, airstrip, and port facilities for watercraft of the Mobile Riverine Force.

Change the jungle

Operation Ranch Hand

WHEN IT COMES to tackling Mother Nature, no job is too big for the US Army Corps of Engineers. Prior to Vietnam, the Corps had a century and a half of overcoming daunting tasks. In the 20th century alone, Army engineers had tamed the mighty Mississippi and Missouri Rivers, dug the Panama Canal, managed the Manhattan Project to develop the atom bomb, and built the Burma Road and Alcan Highway.

Clearing the jungle areas of Vietnam was a small task by comparison. But it was a job no less necessary, and vital to the security of American troops.

Like the dark, the jungle provided cover for the VC and NVA. Roads through the jungle were those most vulnerable to mining and ambush. Jungle areas were tailor-made for concealing enemy bases and supply dumps.

Although the Engineers were also responsible for "clearing of fields of fire. . .clearing and grubbing of troop areas" and "field fortifications," it was land clearing that had priority. It was considered a tactical job that would make more immediate impact on operations than other tasks like base development and airfield construction. But the engineers had not been required to clear heavy jungle for a quarter-century, since the Pacific campaigns of World War II. Old lessons had to be relearned and new equipment developed to clear the jungle.

One of the most effective of the new machines, but also the most ungainly, was the LeTourneau Tree Crusher. The land version of this behemoth weighed more than 60 tons and moved on three, huge, knife-edged wheels. Each wheel was propelled by its own diesel engine. The crusher pushed down trees in its path, then shredded them into

sticks which were pressed into the ground beneath
it. A 100-ton version called the transphibian tactical
tree crusher was used in swampy areas. Effective
as it was in destroying the jungle, the LeTourneau
Tree Crusher—like the dinosaur—became a victim
of its own size. In the jungle it proved a vulnerable
target with complex machinery that required con-
siderable maintenance. When it broke down in the
jungle, it was too big to be extracted smoothly.

Far more preferable as a land clearing device for
tactical use was the Rome Plow, which quickly
became the workhorse of the jungle-stripping teams.
It was a standard bulldozer tractor on an Allis-
Chalmers HD16 or Caterpillar D7E chassis with a
heavy-duty cab built up to protect the operator from

falling trees. The secret of its success—and the source of its nickname—was the huge tree-cutting blade made by the Rome Company of Georgia.

Mounted in place of the usual bulldozer blade, the giant Rome K/G Clearing Blade had a leading edge that was honed frequently to keep it knife-sharp. On the 4,600-pound blade's lower left front corner was mounted a rigid spike, or "stinger." The blade was canted slightly to the right to throw debris aside and not block the bulldozer's progress.

As the Rome Plow sliced into the jungle, the blade stayed about 6 inches off the ground, shearing through the vegetation but leaving the roots in place, to prevent erosion. Thicker trees were tackled by repeated stabbing with the stinger and turning

TREES TO MATCHSTICKS: With the ease of a combine harvester cutting corn, a tree crusher shreds and clears a swath of jungle. The 60-ton giant first bulldozed trees in its path, then used its massive bulk to crush them.

the dozer to wrench and wrestle the trunk fibers apart.

After field tests in late 1966 proved the Rome Plow's effectiveness, Westmoreland's staff immediately ordered 100 Plows, which the engineers quickly put into action in the jungle. Eventually, Westmoreland said, he ended up with more than 1,000 because they worked so well.

The first major test of the Plows came in the Iron Triangle, an enemy enclave close to the capital Saigon and scene of the bloody battles of Operation Cedar Falls in January 1967. General Westmoreland would later write that "the Rome Plows carved great hunks from the jungle and worked round and round the circumference until they reduced trees and brush to combustible rubbish, leaving the guerrillas no place to hide."

Formed at first into land-clearing platoons of 30 Plows each, the units had more work than they could handle. So many commanders made calls on their services that commitment of Rome Plows became a matter for high level control. By the summer of

1967, ninety Rome Plows were in operation. With only 64 men for 30 tractors, the manning of the early land-clearing platoons was sparse. Soon the platoons were expanded into company-sized units of 132 men. At that size, the land-clearing companies were more self-sufficient, better able to perform field repairs needed to keep operating.

Repair and maintenance was essential. General Robert Ploger, commander of the US Army Engineer Command in 1966-67, reported that one-half to two-thirds of the Rome Plows suffered disabling damage every day of operation. It was routine for a plow operator to spend 12 hours clearing jungle, then return to the night defensive position and work for 6-8 hours more in the darkness repairing his tractor. All that work, said General Ploger, "for the honor of being able to repeat the cycle on the following day."

In a typical day, a land-clearing company could clear 150-200 acres of medium jungle working alongside a security force composed, ideally, of a mechanized infantry company riding shotgun on M-113 armored personnel carriers. At the end of the day the M-113s and the Plows would circle wagons into a hastily assembled night defensive position, before sallying forth the next day to denude their assigned chunk of jungle.

THE DROP:
A huge CH-54 "Flying Crane," capable of lifting up to 20,000 pounds, hooks a bulldozer into a clearing to begin construction of LZ Wainwright north of Tay Ninh. Airlifting was the preferred method for heavy equipment as South Vietnam's limited and poorly constructed road network was subject to mines and ambushes.

Change the jungle

STRIPPED EARTH:
"Rome Plow" blades fitted to standard bulldozers and cutting at just above ground level speared and slashed their way through the jungle. An engineer company of Rome Plows could clear 150-200 acres of jungle per day. The clearance rate fell when they encountered hazards that could include enemy land mines and swarms of bees.

Night defensive positions were moved every few days as the area was cleared. Staying too long in one place invited enemy attacks, and unnecessarily lengthened the journey out to the area to be cleared.

Navigation inside the dense triple-canopy jungle was a problem at first. It was solved by equipping the leading Rome Plow with a radio, so that its operator could receive directional guidance from a helicopter flying overhead. Other Rome Plows in the unit fanned out from the leader in an echelon formation to maintain the proper heading. Once a perimeter was cut delineating the area to be shaved,

the helicopter was no longer necessary. Slashing through the jungle in ever-decreasing perimeter swaths, the tractors chugged round and round until the jungle was cleared.

Enemy action was an ever-present hazard with most combat casualties inflicted by land mines and night mortar attacks.

Natural hazards, such as falling trees, contributed to the casualty lists. Swarms of bees were often kicked up by the clearing, sometimes attacking so fiercely that they completely halted work and forced the the stricken operators to evacuate.

FILL 'ER UP:
A routine scene at Da Nang air base in 1966 as ground crewmen pump defoliant spray into the tanks aboard a USAF C-123 transport of Operation Ranch Hand. No precautions were taken to prevent the men from accidentally, inhaling or ingesting Agent Orange, which had been used for defoliant spraying missions since 10 January 1962.

Driving a Rome Plow was frontline work and almost as hazardous as the life of a grunt in an infantry platoon. According to General Ploger's casualty statistics, two-thirds of the operators became casualties from enemy action during their tour. Nevertheless, the Rome Plow operators maintained a high esprit and reenlisted or extended their tours in Vietnam at an extraordinarily high rate.

Because land clearing had such a high priority, higher authorities were interested in the daily production reports from Rome Plow companies. Competition between units was keen. Usually they reported 150-200 acres a day of jungle cleared away.

But one company commander was best remembered for his forthright report one muddy monsoon day. On the line for "acres cleared," he wrote, "one tree." Headquarters questioned the report. It transpired that the company had become mired in the monsoon mud en route to the clearing area. The sole tree they felled was because a plow operator tied his winch cable to a dead tree to become unstuck. When he applied power, the tree fell over.

DEFOLIATION AND CROP DENIAL are bland terms. But the programs performed under those names tinkered with Nature in ways yet unclear, two decades removed.

The stimulus for the defoliation program was the constant need to cut the enemy from his cover—the protective screen of the jungle. Crop denial aimed

to keep food out of enemy mouths, particularly rice crops in VC-controlled areas.

The weapons of both these programs were chemical defoliants. The need for such programs had first been established by US advisers in the early 1960s. In 1961 President Kennedy had approved establishment of Project Agile, a test center in Vietnam to examine tactics and techniques for counterinsurgency. One of the ideas Project Agile tested was spraying defoliants from the air to cut jungle growth along highways where ambushes were frequent.

Early in 1962, Air Force crews flying C-123 Provider transports began test defoliation flights along the highway between Bien Hoa and Vung Tau, where heavy jungle provided cover for nightly ambushes and mining. But the spray was mixed too thinly, and it was not effective.

After refining the mixtures and rigging better spray systems on the C-123 aircraft, effective defoliation resulted. The leaves turned brown, dried up, and fell off.

RANCH HAND: During spraying operations C-123 transport aircraft spraying herbicides and defoliants flew in echelon formation at extremely low levels (100 feet), to dispense spray at a rate of 3 gallons per acre. One plane could cover an area 80 meters wide and 16 kilometers long.

DEADLY MIST: From inside a Ranch Hand C-123 aircraft, the mist from its spray booms settles over dense jungle. One thousand gallons of liquid defoliant were pumped into the nozzles in the spray booms that dispersed the defoliant as mist.

Operation Ranch Hand was under way, using commercially available herbicides and dessicant chemicals. Relatively unknown outside the agrichemical business in 1962, the agents used quickly entered the vocabulary. Two agents most frequently sprayed were Blue and Orange, named after the colored identifying stripes on their containers.

Agent Orange is now in Webster's Dictionary. Webster's definition reads: "an herbicide widely used as a defoliant in the Vietnam War that is composed of 2,4-D and 2,4,5-T and contains dioxin as a contaminant." Dioxin is one of several hydrocarbons occurring as persistent toxic impurities in herbicides, according to Webster's. By definition a herbicide is a chemical which will kill or injure a plant when applied to air, soil, water, or the plant

itself. Defoliants cause the leaves of a plant to fall prematurely.

Agent Blue is a dessicant, a drying agent. It works on contact. Plant tissues touched by Agent Blue dry up and drop off. However, the plant itself is not necessarily killed. That depends on the concentration of the mixture, health of the plant, and weather conditions. New leaves may grow back within 30-90 days after an application of Agent Blue.

Agent Orange kills plants, being classified as a systemic herbicide. It interferes with the plant's growth processes such as photosynthesis. It was sprayed by chemical platoons in tactical units on foliage around fire bases. The small quantities used had immediate tactical value in improved observation and in clearing fields of fire. Any large-scale

HIDDEN RISKS: A Ranch Hand spray pilot checks the nozzles of the spray boom rigged below the aft fuselage of his C-123 transport. Spray missions were usually flown in the early hours of the morning when the wind was near calm. Little or no precautions were taken by those handling the principal defoliant, Agent Orange, which was then thought to be harmless. Only later would servicemen exposed to Agent Orange realize the risk they ran of having children born with congenital defects because of that exposure.

spraying was assigned to USAF C-123 aircraft and the crews of Operation Ranch Hand.

To get approval for a Ranch Hand spray mission was a complicated and lengthy process. For political reasons, the use of herbicides for defoliation was deemed a South Vietnamese government operation that the US supported. Authority for US support was exercised at the top by the so-called "country team," consisting of the US Ambassador to Vietnam and the Commander of US Military Assistance Command Vietnam (MACV).

Requests for defoliation and crop-spraying missions started with Vietnamese district and province chiefs. The requests then flowed through two channels. On the ARVN side, they went to division and corps tactical zones. On the American side US district and province advisers transmitted their views on to MACV's Operations Directorate (J-3).

Both the US and Vietnamese sides had a "203 Committee" for coordinating the chemical spraying requests. After coordination and staffing, the Ambassador and MACV commander gave approval. Then the word went back down both chains of command and to Ranch Hand units for planning. The final assignment and precise timing of a spray mission was determined by other priorities; the aircraft available and rival requests for bombing missions that were more urgent. Approved spray missions were "on order," to be flown when directed. A province chief had the option of canceling a spray mission at the last moment, 24 hours before it was flown. If he did not do so, the C-123s flew the mission.

Aboard each C-123 was a 950-gallon tank containing the herbicide, and pumps to push it up and out into the spray booms under wings and tail. When they reached the target area, the aircraft flew in echelon formation at about 150 feet above ground level. At such low altitudes and flying at a relatively slow airspeed of 140 knots, the large converted transport aircraft were vulnerable to ground fire and engine failure. Forward air controllers and fighter-bombers were available on call to protect the spray aircraft from ground fire, but nothing could prevent engine failure.

Approaching a target area, a mission commander took into account the wind direction and speed, as well as identifying areas not to be sprayed. Herbicide was then pumped from the tanks into the spray booms and forced out of apertures, finer than the holes in a shower head. When the fluid hit the slipstream, its drops broke into finer droplets, creating a spray mist that settled onto the foliage below.

President Gerald R. Ford —When the real price of using Agent Orange began to emerge, he renounced the future use of such chemical weapons.

The spray from each aircraft covered a swath about 300 feet wide. Concentrated at about 3 gallons per acre, an aircraft could carry enough to cover more than 300 acres per mission.

Ranch Hand crews flew more than 19,000 sorties from 1962 to 1968. The operation peaked in 1967. Nearly 1,500,000 acres of forest and 200,000 acres of crops were sprayed. Crop spraying dropped off sharply after 1967 to about 50,000 acres in each of the next two years. Forest spraying continued at 1,250,000 acres per year—roughly equivalent to annually destroying an area the size of the state of Delaware—during 1968 and 1969. In the ready room at Operation Ranch Hand General Westmoreland noted the sign that would have shocked ecologists. It read, "Only You Can Prevent Forests."

Then in April 1970, the Defense Department banned the use of Agent Orange, and by July 1970 all fixed-wing defoliation spraying was halted. Crop destruction missions stopped soon after.

Controversy over the defoliation campaign began about the same time it started, and continues today. The tactical value of defoliation in the immediate area of fire bases was clear. No one doubted that it contributed to troop safety. However, the virtues of large-scale defoliation and crop destruction were open to question from the start.

The first opposition came in 1964, only two years after the spraying began, when members of the Federation of American Scientists accused the US of experimenting in biological and chemical warfare. Their objections were brushed aside. Harder to ignore was a petition presented to President Johnson's science adviser in February 1967, signed by more than 5,000 scientists, including 17 Nobel laureates and 129 members of the National Academy of Sciences. Nor could the administration ignore a call from the American Association for the Advancement of Science (AAAS) demanding studies of the short and long-term consequences of using pesticides and herbicides on such a large scale.The Defense Department commissioned such a study, which suggested at the end of 1967 that the long-term consequences were unresolved questions.

With such uncertainty, and with general opposition to the war spreading after the Tet Offensive in 1968, large-scale use of defoliants and herbicides became more unpopular among a wider slice of the populace. It is not surprising, therefore, that Presidents Nixon and Ford would eventually restrict and then end the programs.

In Vietnam the US Ambassador, Ellsworth Bunker, established a Herbicide Review Committee in January 1968 to review the program. It recognized the military value of defoliation, but the committee also noted the economic and psychological costs of the program. The most tangible economic loss it pinpointed was the destruction of

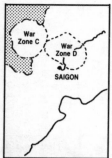

War Zones C and D —In 1968 these heavily forested Viet Cong strongholds were regularly sprayed. Captured VC questioned about the effects of defoliation confessed that they avoided crossing recently sprayed areas and would not camp in them.

hardwood timber in War Zones C and D. In the psychological arena, Ranch Hand gave the VC and NVA the opportunity to accuse the US of resorting to chemical warfare. Bunker's committee regarded crop destruction as potentially counterproductive since the civilian population bore the brunt of the program's effects, with resulting adverse political and psychological costs.

Hardwood forests suffered most from the spray programs. A Congressional report in 1971 estimated that 35 percent of South Vietnam's 14 million acres of hardwood forests had been sprayed at least once and about one-half of the coastal mangrove forests (750,000 acres) had been totally destroyed.

An early question was whether the defoliated areas could regenerate if left alone. Department of Agriculture experts summoned to survey the forests in 1968 failed to reach any conclusion. One of the experts, Fred H. Tchirley, reported that the spray program had caused ecological changes. He did not believe the changes were irreversible, but that recovery could take a long time, 20 years in the case of the mangroves. He found it harder to reach a

THE PRICE:
The long, light, straggling bald patch down the center of the Que Son Valley, southwest of Da Nang, represents the brown, lifeless zone created by spraying with Agent Orange. The dark patches on the hills either side are the green forests that escaped the spray missions.

diagnosis regarding the semideciduous hardwood forests. The regeneration time scale was unknown, and available information was "so scanty that a prediction would have no validity and certainly no real meaning," he said.

Then, little attention was paid to the long-term effects on humans of the dioxin component in Agent Orange. At the time it was not possible for scientists conclusively to attribute stillbirths and birth defects in sprayed areas to the herbicides. And no one was speculating on the long-term effects upon American airmen who handled the herbicides or soldiers who tramped through affected areas. In 1988, those questions are still being probed, continuing an effort begun in Congress in October 1970.

President Gerald R. Ford announced US policy on future use of herbicides and riot control agents in war in Executive Order 11850, signed on 8 April 1975. On herbicides, EO 11850 read:

"The United States renounces, as a matter of national policy, first use of herbicides in war except use, under regulations applicable to their domestic use, for control of vegetation within US bases and installations or around their immediate defense perimeters. . . ."

The policy clearly prohibits future operations like Ranch Hand.

As for the stocks of Agent Orange that remained, the 1,370,000 gallons remaining in Vietnam were removed to remote Johnston Island in the Pacific before April 1972. An additional 850,000 gallons were stored in the US at Gulfport, Mississippi. The Air Force was directed to dispose in accordance with environmental standards and without creating additional problems. Eventually, after nearly six years of test and evaluation, incineration far at sea was chosen as the method of disposal. A furnace-equipped ship, the *Vulcanus*, was the means. On 3 September 1977, the last bit of Agent Orange was burned in the North Pacific.

Definitive conclusions have still not been reached on the long-term health effects of the chemicals sprayed in Vietnam. The US Air Force has conducted a long-term study to compare the health of 1,200 Ranch Hand veterans with a control group of similar men. That study continues in 1988.

At the same time, the Veterans Administration

Tight pattern —Four Ranch Hand C-123s flying in tight echelon lay down a carpet of defoliant over 300 meters wide. Concern about the effect of herbicide drift led to improved operational procedures with missions flown just after dawn when the wind was lightest.

THE DAISY CUTTER

A CH-54 Flying Crane helicopter prepares to lift a 10,000-pound "Daisy Cutter" bomb capable of clearing a section of jungle or destroying enemy bunkers and minefields in one blast. The Daisy Cutter consisted of the ultra-heavy BLU-82/B bomb and a point-detonating (PD) fuse. The bomb was too big to fit in, or under, most bombers. Instead it was either rolled out of the cargo ramp of the C-130 Hercules or carried under a CH-54 Flying Crane helicopter. For the Daisy Cutter the PD fuse was specially extended by a metal rod about 3 feet long. At the point of impact this kept the nose of the bomb 3 feet off the ground. When the PD reacted, the bomb's tremendous force was radiated outward instead of into the ground. Thousands of heavy chunks of twisted steel slashed through everything within a 50-meter radius, turning jungle into matchsticks and creating an instant LZ up to 100 meters in diameter.

and other agencies have been evaluating the cases of Vietnam veterans who believe that their latent medical complaints are the result of exposure to Agent Orange.

Lawyers for groups of veterans have brought class action suits against the government and manufacturers of the chemicals used in Operation Ranch Hand. However, on the narrow legal questions the courts refused to hold the manufacturers liable and determined the government was immune from the suits. Five of the major manufacturers set up a fund of $180 million for relief of veterans. In early 1988, the class action cases were on appeal to the Supreme Court. The story of Agent Orange and Operation Ranch Hand is still not closed.

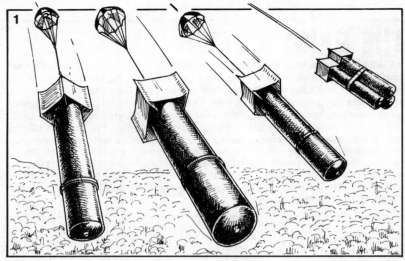

THE SUPER PRESSURE BOMB

THE MOST DIABOLICALLY EFFECTIVE device for blasting away the jungle was Fuel Air Explosive (FAE). US Navy scientists began work on FAE in 1966. The principle of FAE is to create a concentrated aerosol mist over the target, then cause it to explode. Enormous blast overpressures of up to 300 pounds per square inch (psi) were created, blasting away everything and anything within its lethal radius. (Normal atmospheric pressure, that is, the pressure on earth, is 14.7 psi, and a conventional bomb blast creates pressure close to 20 psi.)

In its first combat test against a minefield in 1967, FAE produced spectacular results. FAE munitions developments were closely kept secrets as development pressed ahead. In 1969-70, the operational FAE bomb designated CBU-55 was tested.

The CBU-55 is a free-fall cluster bomb unit carrying three 100-pound canisters of liquid ethylene oxide. After dropping from a slow-flying aircraft, the canisters separate and their fall is delayed by drogue parachutes.

When they hit the ground, the containers rupture and the ethylene oxide becomes a cloud of vapor about 15 meters in diameter and 2.5 meters high. A delayed action igniter detonates the vapor cloud, which explodes to create immediate intense blast overpressures up to 300 psi.

In action in Vietnam, a single CBU-55 could completely defoliate an area of jungle 30 meters in diameter within a matter of seconds.

Find the enemy

4

The coming of the electronic battlefield

PRESIDENT JOHNSON'S Rolling Thunder bombing campaign against North Vietnam in 1965-66 progressed through three distinct phases, beginning with attacks against the transportation system. When this campaign of interdiction failed to bring the North to the conference table, Washington escalated the campaign with attacks against North Vietnam's oil storage installations. The premise was that knocking out oil storage sites would hamper the North's ability to send materials south and bring about negotiations.

In the third phase, LBJ authorized striking previously sacrosanct "war-supporting facilities" such as an airfield, power plants, and ammunition dumps. The next phase began in April 1968 with a bombing halt north of the 20th Parallel.

Despite the policy gyrations reflected in LBJ's different approaches to bombing the North, the results could not be dodged. That is, the bombing campaigns did not sap North Vietnamese will; nor cause Hanoi to sue for peace; nor stop the massive flow of men and supplies to the conflict in the South.

Frustrated at the lack of tangible results from the bombing, the then Secretary for Defense, Robert S. McNamara, proved receptive when one of his senior civilian deputies, John McNaughton, early in 1966 floated the idea for an electronic barrier that would separate North and South Vietnam. The basic concept had come from Professor Roger Fisher of Harvard Law School.

McNamara, who had been appointed by Kennedy in 1961 and had overseen the escalation of US strength in Vietnam, was perturbed by the direction that US involvement was taking. In the summer of 1966 he had convened a senior group of academics,

Find the enemy

MCNAMARA'S FENCE:

Known as the McNamara Line, this electronic fence was to run along the 160 miles of the DMZ to detect and prevent enemy infiltration. For a few months in 1966, Defense Secretary Robert McNamara and his advisers were convinced that this unmanned line of fixed sensors and obstacles, backed up by men in fortified positions a few miles to the south, could finally solve the problem of controlling the DMZ. The fence was never completed. But the technology it would have used was employed in numerous situations.

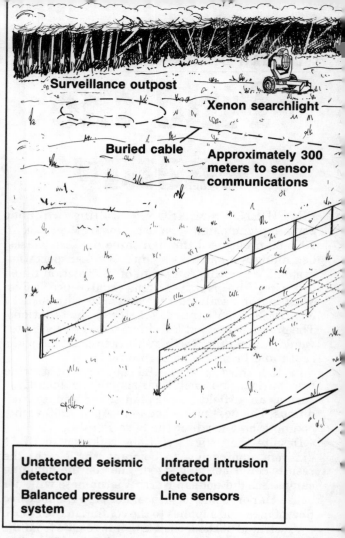

Surveillance outpost

Xenon searchlight

Buried cable

Approximately 300 meters to sensor communications

Unattended seismic detector

Infrared intrusion detector

Balanced pressure system

Line sensors

under the code name "Jason," to evaluate the US conduct of the war. Among the topics they scrutinized in utmost secrecy was the bombing campaign and Fisher's notion of the electronic barrier.

Their recommendations led to the McNamara Line, or Electric Fence. It was to be a physical barrier across the Demilitarized Zone (DMZ) between North and South. Until then the DMZ was just a line on a map running roughly along the 17th Parallel with supposedly "neutral" zones either side. Established by the Geneva Accords peace process of 1954, the DMZ was the effective border between the

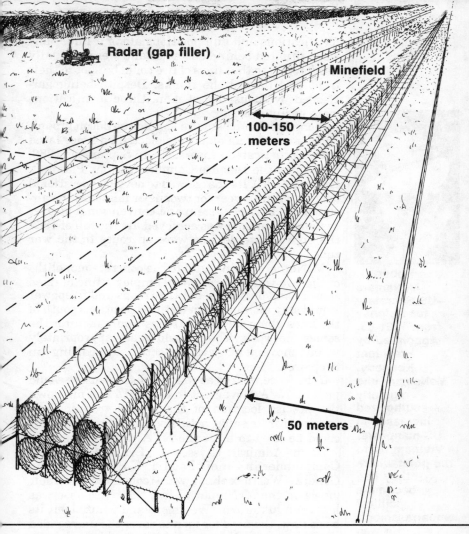

Radar (gap filler)

Minefield

100-150 meters

50 meters

newly created two Vietnams. The notion under-pinning the McNamara line was that if men and supplies could not be located or destroyed by an aerial bombing campaign against the North, then the electric fence would stop them being moved south.

The top secret project was given the code name Dye Marker. The Jason group warmed to it and en-visioned a line of obstacles and sensors, stretching 160 miles from the sea along the DMZ and into Laos. In World Wars I and II, fortified lines like the Siegfried or Maginot Lines had used fixed heavy

Robert S. McNamara —US Secretary for Defense from 1961-68. Appointed by President Kennedy, McNamara had regularly authorized increases in US manpower in Vietnam up to the point where they had become a political embarrassment. He was attracted to the notion of the electronic fence, named after him, because it promised to save manpower.

fortifications and gun positions along a line. They were situated behind obstacles and were mutually reinforcing, so that lines of fire could be shot to their front and toward the flanks. Despite being garrisoned by thousands of men, these fortifications were easily overrun.

Nonetheless McNamara shared the Jason group's enthusiasm for an elaborate electrified fence laced with sophisticated sensors. On 15 September 1966, he formed the Defense Communications Planning Group (DCPG). Its charge was to develop operational devices within a year for two major missions: the air-supported barrier system and conventional barrier systems. That goal was achieved. By the fall of 1967 the appropriate devices were en route to the war zone .

McNamara's Line, unlike the concrete monoliths of the two world wars, would employ a line of fixed sensors and obstacles, but the troops and firepower would stay mobile. From fortified positions south of the lines along the DMZ, troops would monitor the sensor network. They would react appropriately when movement was detected by calling in firepower.

If the fence worked as conceived, the sensors would pick up NVA movement in the DMZ and pin down the precise location of the enemy troops. Then firepower from ships, artillery, and tactical aircraft could be used to blast the NVA in their tracks.

When Admiral Ulysses S. Grant Sharp, the Commander-in-Chief Pacific (CINCPAC), and General Westmoreland were consulted for their views on the McNamara Line, their response was less than lukewarm. Westmoreland pointed out its basic flaw, the need for men to cover the unattended electronic gear. He estimated it would tie down a battalion every mile or so. Admiral Sharp believed it would tie up 20,000 combat troops better used in fighting farther south in South Vietnam.

But in Washington, where the rising numbers of US troops being sent to Vietnam was fast becoming a political embarrassment, economy of force was seen as one of its virtues. US and ARVN troops operating in the DMZ or immediately south of it had proved especially vulnerable to well-aimed North Vietnamese mortars and artillery fired from just across the border. The fence would cut down the need for continuous patrolling by men, substituting thousands of sensors for flesh and blood. One general summarized the Line's purpose as "making enemy movement across the DMZ simultaneously more expensive for the attacker and less expensive for the defender."

At that time, the very existence of the sensors was a closely held secret. Sensors were held in awe—truly wondrous gadgets that would change the way wars were fought. Instead of men risking their lives to find the enemy, the sensors would do it. Men remote from the scene would evaluate the information from the sensors, and bring firepower down on the enemy. This was the genesis of the "electronic battlefield."

In practice the Line would still be a tangle of buried wires and sensors capable of being activated in several ways. The balance pressure system reacted to an increase in weight, whenever a person stepped on it. Infrared intrusion detectors picked up movement whenever a beam of infrared energy, invisible to the human eye, was interrupted. Seismic detectors picked up vibrations from footfalls, such as a platoon of troops walking along a trail. Acoustic sensors reacted to noise. When enemy troops stepped on small explosive devices, the popping noise kicked off the acoustic sensor.

An elaborate system of buried wires led from the sensors back to surveillance outposts. In the outposts, men watched and listened for indications from the sensors, whose locations were plotted precisely on their situation maps.

Construction of the electric fence began in April 1967. By then, the flow of North Vietnamese units and supplies from north to south had increased substantially. General Westmoreland reacted by shifting US Marine units northward inside the I Corps area to build up strength in the area immediately south of the DMZ.

The buildup of the Marines and enemy activities elsewhere diverted attention away from the McNamara Line. North Vietnamese units along the DMZ reacted predictably to its construction. Their rockets and artillery interfered with the work. Throughout the rest of 1967 the US troop buildup in the northern provinces intensified. Demands for supplies and ammunition burgeoned. The logistic

Admiral Ulysses S. Grant Sharp —Commander-in-Chief Pacific and responsible to Washington for the Vietnamese theater of war. Along with General Westmoreland he succeeded in getting the McNamara Line permanently shelved.

Find the enemy

AIR-DELIVERY:
An airman prepares to drop a Phase I Air-Delivered Seismic Detection Sensor (ADSID) over the Ho Chi Minh Trail during operation Igloo White. The delivery method was crude but effective. Dropped like a giant lawn dart, the 25-pound ADSID buried itself 30 inches deep leaving only its antenna visible. The ADSID was triggered by ground vibrations, and was sensitive enough to distinguish between the footfall of a man walking and the rumble of a truck.

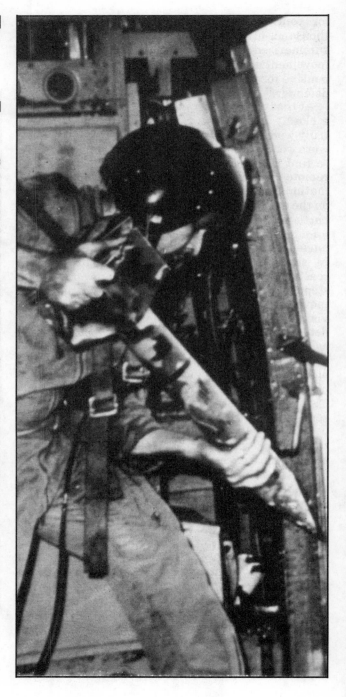

support system could not serve both the troop buildup and the electronic fence construction. The McNamara Line was quietly put on the shelf. Parts of it had progressed far enough to turn over to ARVN units along the DMZ. That freed US Army and Marine troops for mobile operations.

But the McNamara Line did not disappear without trace. Sensors and the concept they embodied were used in countless locations such as fire bases and surveillance sites. The most notable diversion of sensors from the line was for the siege of Khe Sanh from January to April 1968.

The Marines at that beleaguered border outpost hunkered under a cold, low overcast that hung on the hills and lifted only slightly during the day. They were the bait in a trap to lure the enemy into concentrating large numbers into attacking Khe Sanh so that he could then be pulverized by air strikes and artillery. The Marines at the base were not numerous enough to patrol outside the base and its nearby outposts. They were truly besieged.

On 18 January, General Westmoreland decided to divert the highly secret sensors from the McNamara Line to the area around Khe Sanh. As the NVA buildup developed, it was clear that there would be plenty of targets for the artillery and airpower being massed in support of the isolated base. The challenge was to locate them precisely and in time to smash them with hot steel before they overran the 26th Marine Regiment hunkered down in their reinforced holes inside the combat base.

Within a few days of Westmoreland ordering the diversion of the sensors to Khe Sanh, the Air Force had sown 250 acoustic and seismic sensors at the most promising locations. Once movement was detected, whether by the sound of a vehicle engine or the tread of sandal on a trail, the sensor's battery was activated so that it could transmit a signal to a relay aircraft 20,000-25,000 feet overhead. The aircraft orbiting over Khe Sanh relayed the signal across Laos and down into the Infiltration Surveillance Center (ISC) at Nakhon Phanom (NKP) on the west bank of the Mekong in Thailand.

Inside the ISC, signal data from the sensors was fed into computers programmed for a surveillance program known as Igloo White. The computers compared the new signals with known signals, and

Calibrating —A target acquisition radar of the 26th Artillery is calibrated for spotting enemy movement inside the Demilitarized Zone.

displayed the results on screens for analysts to piece together. Their deductions on the type of target that was causing the sensors to react, and the target's coordinates, were then radioed back to the fire support coordination center at Khe Sanh.

Target type and location were all the information the Marine fire support coordinators needed. With that, they called down artillery, fighter-bombers, or B-52 Arc Light bombers on targets, never seen but only sensed by unmanned automatons.

In the first few days of using sensors it rapidly became apparent that firing at every movement for which data existed was a fast way to waste ammunition. Better results were achieved when the analysts integrated sensor information with other indicators to work out where the enemy was massing.

Find the enemy

NERVE CENTER:
At the heart of operation Igloo White, the electronic surveillance and interdiction of enemy movement along the Ho Chi Minh Trail, was the Infiltration Surveillance Center (ISC) at Nakhon Phanom on the west bank of the Mekong in Thailand. The windowless air-conditioned complex was tucked away in a jungle clearing and off-limits to everyone but the analysts who worked there. It was here that sensor signals, relayed by aircraft, were processed by computers and displayed on-screen for analysts to construct a picture of enemy movements.

If sensor data was used much of the time for filling in the gaps in the intelligence picture, it did, on one occasion, have to provide the whole picture—filling the void created when the Marines at Khe Sanh went underground and stopped patrolling. However, by this stage the analysts at the Infiltration Surveillance Center at NKP had built up an intimate knowledge of the area around Khe Sanh and the patterns of enemy activity.

But it was as a complement to other intelligence that sensor data was at its most effective. As the official command history would later state, sensors came into their own in conditions of low visibility providing the " 'now is the time' cue for strikes."

Colonel David Lownds, commanding officer of the 26th Marines, testified to the US Senate about his use of sensors during the Khe Sanh siege. He was

Col. David Lownds —As commanding officer (CO) of the 26th Marines at Khe Sanh he was one of the first combat COs to appreciate the value of sensors in locating and helping to destroy the enemy. He later testified to the US Senate that the sensors at the siege of Khe Sanh had saved lives.

convinced that the use of sensors had saved lives among his Marines. It was difficult to assign a precise number, but Lownds thought that casualties would have been twice as high without the sensors. Assault troops from the NVA divisions pressing on Khe Sanh would have been able to get inside the Marine positions and double the casualties, he testified.

On the future implications of sensors, he said, "The actual battlefield of the future won't be that much different from the past. The red mud of Khe Sanh in 1968 was very much like the mud of Flanders in 1918 to the young men living and fighting in it. The sensor and electronic battlefield as it existed at Khe Sanh were (sic) an extremely valuable adjunct to the defense."

Later in the war, Dr. Eugene Fubini, a senior Defense Department scientist, would claim that, "We have sensors that listen to sounds, detect the footsteps of people walking, smell the presence of human beings, and radars that detect trucks; we have moving target indicators in aircraft; we have coherent and noncoherent side-looking radars. We have infrared scanners, image converters, and infrared superheterodynes. We can use all of these sensors in remote-control and remote-reporting systems that we call the 'instrumented battlefield'."

The most comprehensive section of Fubini's "instrumented battlefield" was the elaborate system of sensors and relays used by the US Air Force to interdict movement along the Ho Chi Minh Trail, a series of trails through Laos and Cambodia that formed the North Vietnamese supply network for communist forces in the South.

Put into operation before the McNamara Line, the Igloo White program involved "sowing" several types of sensors from the air into selected areas along the Ho Chi Minh Trail in Laos. When activated, the sensors emitted a signal that was transmitted to an airborne relay station orbiting high over the trail area. Writing later in the *Armed Forces Journal*, one participant claimed: "We wired the Ho Chi Minh Trail like a drugstore pinball machine, and we plugged it in every night."

The first sensors used in Igloo White were known as the ACOUSID and the ADSID. ACOUSID was the acronym for Acoustic Seismic Intrusion Detector.

ADSID meant Air Dropped Seismic Intrusion Detector. Both were refinements and developments of the sonobuoys dropped from aircraft into the sea as part of the Navy's antisubmarine warfare (ASW) program. Both the ACOUSID and the ADSID incorporated a commandable microphone called COMMIKE that could be switched on or off by remote control from an aircraft orbiting overhead. The COMMIKE device meant that hundreds of sensors could be sown along a trail, remain dormant for months, their battery strength conserved, then switched on when enemy movement was suspected in the area.

The first sensors were sown by the Navy. It quickly modified 15 otherwise obsolete P-2 Neptune patrol aircraft that had been used to sow sonobuoys in the ASW program. In November 1967, the Navy sent 12 of the Neptunes, now designated OP-2E, to Southeast Asia to sow sensors.

The earliest missions were flown at low level, and were successful in delivering sensors. But casualties were high. One OP-2E crashed into a mountain, killing all hands. Two more were lost to NVA flak over northern Laos. Four others were hit by flak, but limped to safety. With the Air Force now geared up to sow sensors, the OP-2Es were retired from the battle zone.

For the hazardous job of dispensing sensors over Laos, the Air Force used the F-4 Phantom. An SUU-42 pod was mounted under the F-4's wing, holding 16 sensors. The technique was for the F-4 to sweep in low and fast over the target area, and pop its 16 seismic sensors out in string formation. After falling a short distance, the 25-pound ADSID devices buried their sharp noses in the soil so that only the antenna protruded, looking very much like a small, five-leaf bush.

A similar technique was used for acoustic sensors, except these descended on small parachutes that were intended to be snagged in the trees, leaving the sound-sensitive devices hanging and ready for work. Once the microphones were activated, the sensors began functioning. The battery life of the devices varied, but was approximately 45 days for the ADSIDs and less for the acoustic sensors.

The sensors were put into action on 15 November 1968 as part of Commando Hunt, the operation to

The Ho Chi Minh Trail —Running from North Vietnam through Laos and Cambodia and into South Vietnam, it was the target for Igloo White, especially in southern Laos. The Trail was the enemy's main supply route after US coastal patrols, early in the conflict, severed the sea route by sinking, grounding, and arresting enemy trawlers laden with arms.

interdict enemy traffic moving south along the Trail.

The transmissions from the sensors were relayed to a converted EC-121R Constellation transport flying at 13,000-15,000 feet. The EC-121R's receiving range was several hundred miles. But in practice, when orbiting over northern Laos, the range to the ISC at Nakhon Phanom was seldom more than 100-150 miles. Besides the necessary radio retransmission equipment, the EC-121R contained an evaluation center and command post with controllers aboard the aircraft capable of evaluating sensor data and directing air support against freshly disclosed targets.

What surprised everyone—except the designers—was the fidelity of the acoustic sensors. Analysts aboard the EC-121R aircraft delighted in listening to NVA truck drivers chattering beneath one of their ACOUSIDs. Back in Washington, Air Force witnesses played tapes of the chatter to fascinated members of Congress.

In addition to the EC-121R aerial command centers, unmanned aircraft, operating under the code name Pave Eagle, acted as simple relay stations retransmitting the signals down to an infiltration surveillance center. The attractions of the Pave Eagle program were its low operating cost and low risk in terms of men and equipment. The Pave Eagle aircraft was usually a Beech Debonair slightly modified for longer endurance that could either be flown by a pilot or by remote control from the ground.

The information from the sensors was fed into an IBM 360/40 computer (replaced late in 1968 with the faster IBM 360/65) at the infiltration surveillance center (ISC). The results were then displayed on screen for an Assessment Officer (AO) to study. Lieutenant Colonel George Weiss later described the process in *Armed Forces Journal*:

"A TV-type screen provides the Assessment Officer a map of the section of Laos under his control. Each of the roads used by the North Vietnamese in his area is etched on his screen. As the seismic and acoustic sensors pick up the truck movements their locations appear as an illuminated line of light, called 'the worm', that crawls across his screen, following a road that sometimes is several hundreds of miles away.

MINISID —A mini seismic intrusion device. One of the smallest of the family of seismic intrusion devices the MINISID was triggered by ground vibrations and used mainly in base defenses to warn against intruders.

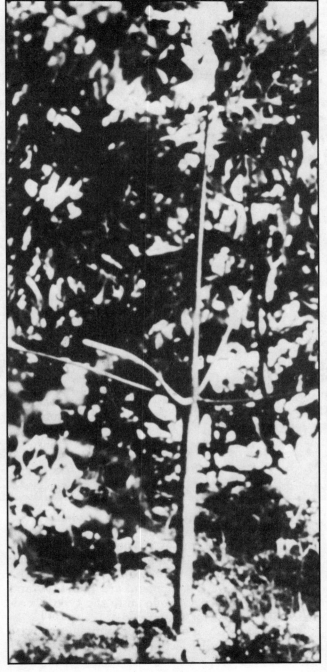

Find the enemy

LISTENING POST:
With only its antenna exposed above ground, this Acoubuoy Sensor was activated by noises. Whatever it picked up was transmitted to an relay aircraft orbiting high overhead. The signals were then relayed to the Infiltration Surveillance Center at Nakhon Phanom, processed, and displayed for action.

"From there the battle becomes academic. The Assessment Officer and the computer confer on probable times the convoy or convoys will reach a pre-selected point on the map. This point is a 'box' selected by the Igloo White team of experts at the ISC. Airborne at the moment are gunships and fighters. A decision is made as to the type of ordnance best suited for the area.

"If the trucks are moving under jungle canopy, it is likely the AO will select fighters armed with CBU type weapons and attack the convoy with them. If

Find the enemy

RADIO RELAY:
High above Laos, EC-121R aircraft like this orbited for eight to ten hours at a time, collecting radio information and relaying signals from ground sensors to the Infiltration Surveillance Center's computers at Nakhon Phanom. INSET: When EC-121Rs could not relay their signals back to the ISC at Nakhon Phanom, or analysis was required closer to the combat zone, this air transportable collection of huts, antennas, and computers called the DART (Deployable Automatic Relay Terminal) was available to interpret sensor information.

the convoy can be caught in an open area, then gunships will be waiting for them."

This was the "electronic battlefield" in its infancy, but showing promise as a means of waging war by remote control. It led Senator Barry M. Goldwater, an Arizona Republican, to eulogize the electronic battlefield as "one of the greatest steps forward since gunpowder."

Relatively modest sums were spent by the DCPG on developing sensors for the electronic battlefield. In its first year, Fiscal Year (FY) 1967, expenditure

Find the enemy

UNMANNED EAGLE: This military version of the civilian Beech Debonair aircraft was known as the Pave Eagle. Unpiloted and operated by remote control, it served as a cheap alternative to the EC-121R airborne relay aircraft for sending signals from the sensor fields along the Ho Chi Minh Trail back to the ISC.

was $330 million. For FYs 1968 and 1969, the sums were $424 and $411 million each, and by FY 1970 the expenditure was down to $213 million.

THE "PEOPLE SNIFFER" was supposed to be the answer to an infantryman's prayer. Called the XM-2 (modified E-63) airborne personnel detector, it was claimed to be able to detect enemy troops by smell even when they were hiding in dense jungle. Field trials in the US suggested the idea had some merit, and the machine was sent to the war zone for testing.

The concept was simple. Sensitive instruments in

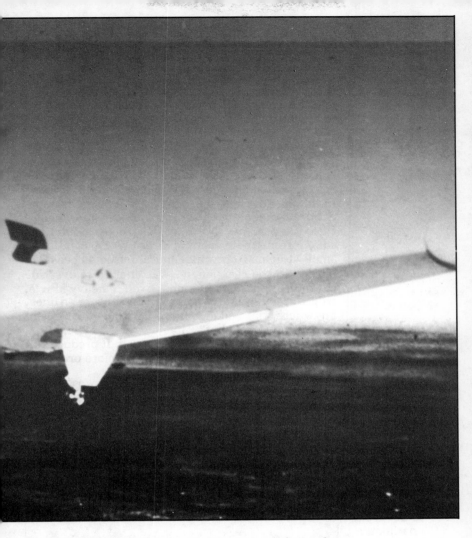

the device would detect certain compounds in the atmosphere. Smoke from campfires, for instance. Or ammonia molecules from human and animal urine, it was said. Because the air in Vietnam was relatively free of pollutants, the tiniest concentrations of smoke or human waste could be detected.

The People Sniffer came to the 196th Light Infantry Brigade west of Tam Ky early in 1968. The device was mounted on a Huey helicopter. In operation, the Huey would scout large areas. Before venturing into assigned reconnaissance areas, the operator calibrated the instruments by flying over villages and camps to make sure the thing was working.

Out in the boonies, the theory went, if the needle flickered there was human activity somewhere upwind. The operator would then direct the helicopter to fly upwind toward the source, find the enemy, and call in the location.

The chemical officer of the 196th Light Infantry Brigade went up on a test mission in the specially rigged helicopter. He quickly discovered that the sniffer was smell sensitive, but unable to discriminate friend from foe. The waste from women, children, and old men caused the same readings as those from armed NVA or VC troops. So did the smoke from their cooking fires. Worst of all, the smell of urine from water buffalo used as beasts of burden in the rice paddies was enough to override the indications from humans. Even in heavy jungle, wild animal waste triggered the sensors. Almost anywhere, the needles jumped with indications of something. But what? That was the problem.

The People Sniffer worked too well. It produced an abundance of false alarms, creating more problems than it solved.

But it was not withdrawn immediately. There are reports of it continuing to be used as late as early 1971 at Long Binh to fly low-level missions over areas of suspected enemy activity. By then, the

SECURITY DEVICE:
—This infrared transmitter was installed by military police at Phu Cat in 1967 to secure a perimeter. Infrared warning devices, triggered by a person breaking the beam, would soon become inexpensive and readily available. In 1967 they represented state-of-the-art security.

PEOPLE SNIFFER: A trooper in the 1st Cavalry Division installs the input-output and probe unit on a Manpack Personnel Detector-Chemical, commonly known as a People Sniffer. It was supposed to be able to detect a person from the chemical compounds in his sweat. But in the field the People Sniffer proved too insensitive —it was unable to distinguish between smells and its meter was frequently overridden by the overpowering smells of animal urine.

drawdown of US troops was in full swing. A helicopter flying very low and slow was a fat target. If shot down, there were fewer combat troops around to go to its rescue. More realistically, the few remaining combat troops were stretched too thin to warrant dispatching them to check out People Sniffer meter readings. Eventually the People Sniffer was retired from active duty.

Automated ambushes

FSBs Floyd and Crook

THE DEFENSE COMMUNICATIONS Planning Group succeeded in its mission of developing unattended sensors for the McNamara Line and Igloo White. In early 1968 its charter was expanded to include development of tactical sensors. The scientists moved quickly to meet the needs of the ground troops, miniaturizing and adapting the existing sensor technology.

For ground tactical use infantrymen received a series of seismic devices that came in three sizes. The largest of the three was the MINISID, but it was still considerably smaller than the 31-inch, 25-pound ADSID dropped by the Air Force on the Ho Chi Minh Trail. Smaller still was the MICROSID, and the PSID was the smallest. PSID stood for Patrol Seismic Intrusion Device.

The PSID was an immediate hit with the grunts. It was small enough to fit into an ammo pouch, so was convenient to carry. The PSID kit consisted of four tiny transmitters and one receiver. Each transmitter was a seismic detector. When a patrol set up a night position or an ambush, the PSIDs were placed on likely approaches to the position. Each of the four transmitters was coded with its own signal. When an enemy approached the patrol, the man monitoring the PSID could tell which one was being activated.

General John R. Deane, Jr., who commanded the 173d Airborne Brigade in 1966-67 and led the DCPG at the time the PSID was developed, stated its value in terms a combat infantryman understood. The PSID was popular with the troops "because it was always alert, never fell asleep," and was reliable. Each PSID cost $280. Early models functioned for about 45 days before wearing out. That was doubled

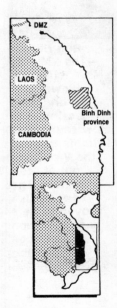

to 90 days on later models, making the device a real bargain.

On an individual basis, each new sensor device improved the tactical ability of units in the combat zone. But it was when ground tactical commanders integrated the new sensors, radars, starlight scopes, and other gadgets into a coherent battle plan, that a true synergy was arrived at and real results achieved. This was forcibly illustrated by two actions—a year apart—at fire bases Floyd and Crook.

The action at Floyd began in the pre-dawn darkness of 29 August 1970, when a battalion of North Vietnamese troops marched smartly along a road in a valley of northern Binh Dinh province. Infiltrating from the sanctuary of Laos not far to the west, the men of 3d Battalion, 2d NVA Regiment were heading for a forward base camp in the hills of Hoai An district. They moved quietly but swiftly, believing their passage safe from American eyes.

Suddenly the dim darkness was lit by the white and red flashes of 4.2-inch and 81mm mortar rounds crashing into the rear of the column. NVA officers urged their men to hurry forward away from the cascade of deadly fire blasting the rear squads and turning the road to rubble. But as they pressed forward, the head of the column was blasted by more mortar rounds landing smack on top of them, reinforced by heavy explosions of 105mm artillery.

The column was trapped between two deadly streams of steel. With daylight approaching, the NVA leaders, now aware that their men could be seen, faced a dilemma. If they stayed in place and fought, they would be pulverized by American mortars and field artillery. With a choice of fight or flee, the NVA commander chose discretion. He ordered his companies to break up into groups of two and three men and flee westward to the relative safety of the mountains.

But even that move was thwarted by US troops. As the NVA troops fled they were pursued by remarkably accurate fire from US mortars, artillery, and concentrated Quad .50 caliber machine guns.

By the time the sun was full up the few NVA troops who had survived the barrage of hot metal had reached the comparative safety of the mountains. Back on the valley floor, all was quiet. Where the 3/2 Battalion had been marching so confidently

Bug Blower —The "Mighty Mite" chemical blower was originally developed to blow smoke and irritants to flush the Viet Cong out of their tunnels. The device also proved to be a handy weapon against bugs around fire bases.

Automated ambushes

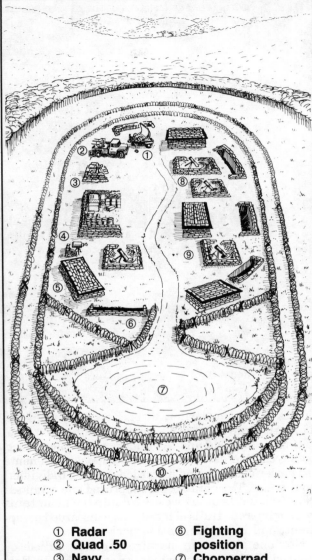

ECONOMY OF FORCE:
The layout for Fire Support Surveillance Base Floyd. Compared to a fire support base, Floyd was lightly defended with only a Quad .50 machine gun and four mortars—two 81mm and two 4.2-inch. But combined with its matrix of radars and sensors constantly tracking the enemy, FSSB Floyd's armaments were sufficient to inflict substantial damage on an NVA regiment.

① **Radar**
② **Quad .50**
③ **Navy binoculars**
④ **Night observation device**
⑤ **Bunker**
⑥ **Fighting position**
⑦ **Chopperpad**
⑧ **81mm mortars**
⑨ **4.2-inch mortars**
⑩ **Perimeter wire**

only a half hour earlier, a reaction force from the 173d Airborne Brigade was now searching the scene. Littering the road and the undergrowth they found bodies of NVA dead, along with weapons, documents in courier pouches, and discarded items of individual equipment. The paratroopers captured one wounded NVA soldier. Leading westward into the mountains were numerous trails of blood, more discarded equipment, and individual ration packs of rice.

Not one American paratrooper was killed or injured in the action, which knocked the 3d Battalion, 2d NVA Regiment out of action for months. The action was a triumph for the planners at Fire Support Surveillance Base (FSSB) Floyd who had integrated sensors and firepower into a well-executed tactical plan.

FSSB Floyd had been established by the 173d Airborne Brigade in "506 Valley" of northern Binh

Dinh province as a means of controlling movement along the corridor that led from the mountains into the populous coastal plain of Binh Dinh. The area was in constant contention between the NVA/VC forces and US troops. Interdiction of 506 Valley was essential to protecting the coastal population.

But by mid-1970, with the US troop withdrawal well under way, the 173d Brigade was spread thin. More than 50,000 US troops had been withdrawn since July 1969 and 50,000 more were due to depart between July and October 1970. Combat units that remained had larger areas to control but fewer men at their disposal. To maintain pressure on the enemy over large areas with fewer troops required what was known as an "economy of force technique."

FSSB Floyd was just that: an economy of force measure to prevent enemy movement in a key area by integrating sensory devices with firepower. The

READY RADAR:
Troopers at a fire support base ready a PPS-5 for night surveillance. The PPS-5 radar was sensitive enough to pick up individual men moving at ranges out to 5,000 meters, and groups of men to 10,000 meters.

HOSE 'EM DOWN: A Quad .50 crew blazes away at an enemy force approaching a fire base in a rare daylight attack. Originally commissioned as an antiaircraft weapon, the Quad .50 proved to be an effective perimeter weapon at fire support bases.

sensors, both attended and unattended, provided early warning and location of enemy troops moving in the area. Once detected and located, the enemy were hit by immediate firepower.

The establishment and operation of FSSB Floyd was a casebook study of the intelligent use of gadgetry at battalion level. In this case the battalion was 3d Battalion, 503d Airborne (3/503), commanded by Lieutenant Colonel Jack B. Farris.

First, 3/503 inserted reconnaissance patrols into the valley to observe and quietly determine the patterns of enemy movement and the locations of base areas. Enemy units operating in the valley or passing back and forth through it were soon identified. They included an NVA regiment, a sapper battalion, part of an NVA artillery battalion, and VC units from the local district.

After 45 days of intense clandestine reconnaissance, the enemy patterns were plotted. The best location for the FSSB was picked and construction began. While the fire base was being constructed, strings of unattended sensors, several hundred feet long, were planted along the known enemy movement routes, sown by air or placed by hand. Most of the work was done at night.

Three types of unattended sensors were placed in strings along preselected routes of movement. Using three types reduced the number of false alarms and provided more data to the men at the FSSB monitoring the valley.

Seismic intrusion devices were basic to all the strings. They reacted to footfalls. Acoustic and magnetic sensors were mixed in with the seismic devices. Because NVA troops tended to talk as they walked, the acoustic sensors reacted to their voices. Magnetic sensors were set off by the weapons and other metal equipment on the enemy soldiers.

The various sensor strings were linked to the Tactical Operations Center (TOC) at FSSB Floyd where operators monitored the strings, awaiting indications they had been triggered. As successive sensors were activated, the TOC operators were able to deduce the direction of movement, the speed, and even the size of the approaching enemy force.

To do something about the discovery required integration of other elements of the base. That meant activating other sensors and fire support.

Because the location of the sensor strings was known precisely, firepower support could be planned with equal precision. Mortar units and artillery teams had prepared fire plans, with elevation and deflection settings calculated for known sensor strings. Sight settings were made for direct-fire weapons such as .50 caliber machine guns and powerful Quad .50s to lay automatic fire on known spots. Sensors were numbered to give the TOC and gunners easy reference to gun data already plotted.

The final elements in the recipe for success at

DIRECT FIRE: With its tube only slightly elevated, a 105mm howitzer fires at attackers closing in on its position. The closer the enemy came, the lower the angle of the tube, until it was horizontal in the mode known as "Killer Junior." This type of close-in final defensive fire usually meant the enemy was in the wire, and a final all-out surge was needed to break the attack, often with the use of Beehive or COFRAM antipersonnel rounds.

Don't Cry —A ROK (Republic of Korea) Tiger Division soldier in protective mask prepares to pop smoke for incoming helicopters. Shortly before the shot was taken, CS tear gas agent had been sprayed on the area to drive away the enemy. CS powder remained potent for several weeks. Any powder left on earth and foliage had the effect of driving the VC from their positions and denying the area to them.

Floyd were its ground radars and visual devices. The PPS-5 radar ranged out to 5 kilometers. Its operators scanned areas around Floyd not covered by the sensors. When something tripped the unattended sensors, the PPS-5 operator swung his scan to the scene to confirm the reading and to maintain contact with the target as it moved.

The major advantages of the PPS-5 radar were that it prevented reaction to false alarms, in tracking fleeing enemy, and in "seeing" through darkness and inclement weather. A PPS-5 operator could provide range and bearing polar coordinates to the TOC and fire direction centers, so that mortars and artillery rounds could smash the enemy even though he had moved out of a sensor field.

Supplementing the PPS-5 radar were two visual devices, the passive TVS-4 Night Observation Device and a set of 20-power naval binoculars. They were additional means of confirming and identifying targets, and maintaining contact with them as they moved about the area.

All this equipment was called into action in the pre-dawn bombardment of 29 August 1970. Lieutenant Colonel Farris recalled that "as the enemy column entered the valley, the southernmost sensor began activating." A sweep by the PPS-5 radar confirmed that an enemy column was heading north in the valley. At the TOC, the decision was to hit the rear of the column first, then try to blast the head of the formation. Farris said, "The rear was hit with mortar fire and, as expected, the remainder of the column marched on."

By now, more sensors in the string were sending information to the TOC. PPS-5 radar continued to track the column, and the TVS-4 night scope had picked up the enemy through the darkness. Howitzers and mortars were laid on a predetermined spot ahead of the enemy column, ready to fire on command. When the head of the column reached that point, it activated the sensor there, and the 173d concentrated its mortar and howitzer fire on the spot.

The enemy broke and began fleeing to the west. As the NVA troops fled, men on the PPS-5 radar and TVS-4 night scopes tracked them. Mortar rounds crumped ahead of the NVA as they scrambled for the hills, and streams of .50 caliber tracers hit them

from behind. Only when the last of the enemy had escaped from the killing zone did the valley fall quiet.

FSSB FLOYD used gadgets in an integrated plan as an economy of force measure. It was a defensive use of sensors and firepower. One year earlier the 25th Infantry Division had used Fire Support Base (FSB) Crook as an offensive site.

Major General Ellis W. Williamson commanded the 25th Division at the time. "Butch" Williamson led the 173d Airborne Brigade into Vietnam in May 1965 and through its first year of campaigning. He urged his officers and men to come up with new solutions to old problems. With that sort of command

encouragement and some lateral thinking, the idea for FSB Crook came about.

FSB Crook was the bait in a trap set to entice the regular 9th VC Division to come across the border from Cambodia to stage one of its massed attacks. The site chosen for FSB Crook was an isolated spot about 9 miles northwest of Tay Ninh City on a known enemy infiltration route from Cambodia toward Saigon.

The site had been traversed by US troops many times before, especially during the big sweeps of Operation Junction City in 1967. And the VC regularly passed by it en route to and from Cambodia. But now it was to be occupied by a small task force of the 25th Infantry Division.

Under the command of Major Joseph E. Hacia, XO (Executive Officer) of the 3d Battalion, 22d Infantry (3/22), FSB Crook's strength consisted of one rifle company, and a battery of six 105mm howitzers plus 81mm and 4.2-inch mortars.

The base was built in a day using rapid construction techniques. First a stake was driven into the ground at the center. A 40-meter rope was attached to the stake and walked around. It established the perimeter of the base, the line where the fighting bunkers were to be built. By using an artillery aiming circle, sites for 24 bunkers were marked every 15 degrees around the perimeter. A 75-meter rope anchored on the center stake now marked the perimeter for the defensive wire barrier.

Next, helicopters flew in with bunker packages—

one for each of the 24 bunkers. Each kit contained demolition charges, steel planking, and sandbags. First the men of 3/22 detonated the shaped demolition charges to create neat craters for their bunker holes. Then they squared off the holes, laid the steel over them, and built sandbag barriers around them.

Inside the perimeter, bulldozers dug out sites for an operation center and medical aid station. Bulldozers around the perimeter pushed up earth to protect the bunkers and artillery and mortar firing positions. Triple concertina wire was unrolled around the perimeter, and hundreds of claymore land mines were placed between the wire and the bunker perimeter. Heavy loads of ammunition for the howitzers and mortars were flown in.

Outside the perimeter, other bulldozers cleared away fields of fire, leaving a few patches of vegetation in the hope that the VC would be enticed to use them for cover. Concentric circles were cut around the base at 150 meters and 300 meters from the center, to be used as range scales for aircraft and helicopters.

The final element was the arrival of a 20-foot prefabricated observation tower flown in by a CH-47 Chinook helicopter. It was deposited in the center of the base. By nightfall the base was ready.

Seismic sensors of several types were installed outside the perimeter under cover of darkness. Inside the base, starlight scopes and ground radar sets were positioned. Artillery units at Tay Ninh and other neighboring bases began computing firing data so that they would be ready to support Crook when

NIGHT READINESS: A trooper sets up his portable AN/PPS-4 ground surveillance radar near Khe Sanh, June 1969. The short-range PPS-4 could detect the movements of individuals and differentiate its signal sufficiently for an experienced operator to determine whether the targets were men or women.

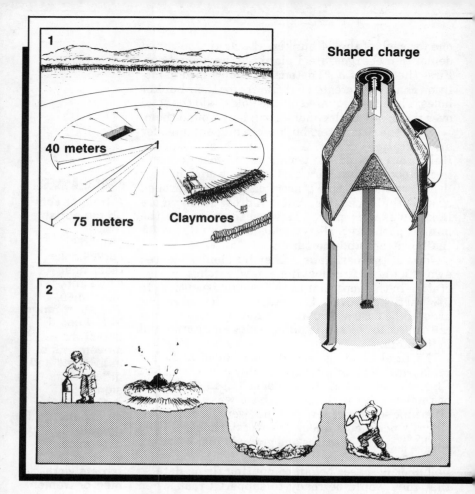

Shaped charge

1

40 meters

75 meters

Claymores

2

needed. Helicopter gunship units and Forward Air Controllers (FACs) reconnoitered the position for the best flight routes, ready for the time when they would be required to provide air support.

The trap was set. Would the 9th VC Division take the bait? The area was quiet throughout the month of May. Patrols from the base found little evidence of enemy presence nearby. Then in early June a normally reliable intelligence source forecast movement of the 272d VC Regiment into the immediate border area.

At FSB Crook on the night of 5 June, the seismic sensors kicked up. Something was moving in the woods less than 1000 meters to the northwest. Ground radar operators picked up signals of other

FASTBUILD

The system that allowed FSB Crook to be built in 24 hours was a refinement of the rapid construction techniques first used in building patrol bases along the Cambodian border.
1. A stake is driven into the center and a 40-meter rope establishes the bunker line, while a 75-meter rope is used to determine the outer wire perimeter.
2. A 15-pound shaped charge explodes, leaving behind a crater to be squared off with a shovel into a 9-foot bunker.
3. A Chinook delivers an already assembled 20-foot observation tower.
4. The location of FSB Crook, 9 miles northwest of Tay Ninh and blocking one of the enemy's favorite infiltration routes from Cambodia. But it was over a month before the NVA accepted the bait.

small groups in the woods. A few rounds of artillery were dropped into the suspected locations, but the enemy movement continued. Major Hacia put the troops into the bunkers and on the guns, at 100 percent alert status. The next move was up to the enemy.

At 0255 hours, a heavy barrage of enemy fire hit FSB Crook. The VC fired rockets, recoilless rifles, rocket-propelled grenades, and mortar rounds into the base. One US soldier was killed in the barrage. As usual, the VC followed the barrage with a ground assault, surging forward with a battalion of troops against the southwest perimeter.

Now the trap was sprung. Gunners on the 105mm howitzers went into the "Killer Junior" mode. Gun

tubes were depressed to the horizontal, and canister and high explosive (HE) rounds were fired at the approaching enemy. Time fuses were set so the rounds exploded 150-200 meters in front of the bunkers. The steel balls and ragged steel fragments scythed through the enemy ranks.

Air Force fighters and helicopter gunships of all kinds flew over the base, pounding the areas outside it with everything in their repertoire. FACs and helicopter pilots counted 15 enemy .51 caliber anti-aircraft machine guns in action, their streams of green tracers arcing into the sky to hit the gunships.

After nearly three hours of pounding, the enemy withdrew. None of the VC soldiers had penetrated the bunker line, although one group blew a hole in the wire with a bangalore torpedo.

The daylight hours of 6 June were quiet. US troops

policed the battlefield, counting 79 enemy bodies, and collecting weapons and documents. After dark, the pattern of the previous night was repeated. Seismic sensors and ground radars detected enemy movement when the attackers were 1,000 meters away from the base. Once again, artillery and mortar rounds were dropped on the enemy movement, which ceased by 0100 hours.

An hour later, a patrolling Nighthawk gunship using his infrared searchlight spotted large groups of enemy soldiers approaching from the east. Supporting artillery was redirected to blast at those formations. As that happened, another heavy enemy barrage slammed into FSB Crook and the VC pressed simultaneous ground assaults from the northwest and northeast. Three US soldiers were wounded in these fights.

Because the attacking enemy were so numerous, more air strikes and helicopter gunships were ordered. Air Force AC-119 and AC-47 Spooky gunships added their lethal load to the steel being dropped on the VC attackers.

From inside the fighting bunkers and gun pits, the men of FSB Crook added their own fires to those of the artillery and air. The few enemy who broke through the concertina wire were blasted by claymores and M-16s before they could breach the bunker line.

BARBED BARRIER:
Better than old-style barbed wire, this steel tape perimeter defense was easier to handle during the setting up of a fire base. One container of barbed tape weighing 40 pounds could be quickly unrolled to create a fence 76 feet long and 30 inches high.

SPECIAL DELIVERY

THE LOW ALTITUDE parachute extraction system (LAPES) was an ingenious solution to the requirement of delivering cargo from a C-130 Hercules transport without landing. In situations where there was no airstrip or the airstrip was under enemy fire, the available options were limited. Try to land, and you risked losing the aircraft and blocking the strip. Drop the equipment by parachute, and it could drift into the enemy positions.

LAPES enabled USAF tactical airlift crews to drop vehicles, ammunition, and supplies with precision under hazardous conditions.

The system was developed in the early 1960s by the Army. Aerial resupply of its forward units was a constant requirement. At the same time the Air Force had its own projects—some quite complex—for delivering gear without parachutes. One system required digging holes on opposite sides of a delivery site. Huge drums were lowered into the holes and filled with water. A short mast bedecked with vanes was then placed in each drum and connected to a cable on reels. The cable was strung across the delivery site. A C-130 transport aircraft would then approach the delivery site at low level (5-10 feet high) with a

By 0530 hours, just before daybreak, the attackers gave up and withdrew into the jungle, pursued by Spooky AC-47 fixed-wing gunships and helicopter gunships. The warm sunlight revealed 363 enemy dead littering the ground outside the perimeter. Ten prisoners were taken, along with 40 weapons and stacks of documents.

That night a few small arms and mortar rounds

load sitting on its rear tailgate. Attached to the load was a hook. This engaged the cable and the load was snatched out of the aircraft. The vanes in the water absorbed the impact of the sudden snatch, preventing the cable from breaking or, worse, the aircraft from being dragged down.

It worked, but was fraught with problems. Holes had to be dug and a water supply found. If the load inside the aircraft was skewed, the hook engaging the cable could bring the plane down with it smack in the middle of an LZ.

By contrast, the boys in the backroom working on the Army's air assault tests had a much simpler approach. Using discarded 15-foot extraction parachutes with a de Havilland C-7 Caribou, a twin-engine high wing transport, the tinkerers at Fort Benning rigged a system that worked. Just as with the C-130, the C-7 Caribou pilot approached the LZ at low level (3-5 feet) with his tailgate down. At the right time, the pilot released the extraction parachute. It fell into the slipstream, popped open, and pulled the load out of the aircraft. At the low level and airspeed (90-100 knots), the load always skidded to a halt undamaged. The scheme was known as LOLEX, for Low Level Extraction.

The Air Force adopted the system, changed the name to LAPES, and used a larger parachute. LAPES was used routinely during the Vietnam War, notably at the siege of Khe Sanh.

were directed at FSB Crook from the jungle, with no damage. The lopsided death toll at FSB Crook for two nights of fighting included 402 men of the VC 272d Regiment killed and 10 captured. 3/22 Infantry suffered one dead and three wounded.

The trap had worked, thanks to a sound plan and the generous use of seismic sensors, starlight scopes, and ground radar.

Command and control

The impact of radio

WHEN AMERICAN ADVISERS went to South Vietnam in the early 1960s, communication experts from the Army Signal Corps were key elements of the team. At that time, security of hamlets and villages was an important part of the overall strategy. That included giving the hamlets some means of telling authorities when their security was threatened. South Vietnam had no civilian telephone system. There was a sparse military telephone network run by the ARVN, but it was unreliable and covered only the main towns and bases. What was needed, but did not exist, was a quick, reliable means of allowing hamlet and village chiefs to be able to warn their district chief when something was wrong, and for him to pass the word to the province chief and so on up the chain of government.

Army doctrine in the early 1960s on fighting a counterinsurgency war was scant to nonexistent. But one of its few booklets on the subject stressed the importance of communications for alerting and calling for help. According to the official Army history of military communications in Vietnam, "the booklet listed many of the primitive but imaginative techniques mentioned in the counterinsurgency plan: drums, flares, balloons, pigeons, and smoke." The signal advisers tried out the techniques recommended in the literature. They soon discovered that what sounded good in theory was hard to practice in the real world. For example, where in a remote hamlet do you find helium for balloons, let alone transport and store it? Or find pigeon feed? The Army tried, however. It trained carrier pigeons at Fort Monmouth, New Jersey, and sent them over to Vietnam for use in carrying messages from isolated

Command and control

UP ANTENNA: American advisers erect the antenna for a 20-watt TR-20, an AM radio that permitted isolated hamlets and villages to communicate with district officials. As Vietnam did not possess a nationwide civilian telephone network, the arrival of the TR-20 was a momentous event in the life of a village, putting it in contact with the outside world for the first time.

hamlets. Unfortunately, says the history, before the pigeons could prove their worth "they succumbed to disease or landed in the cooking pots of hungry South Vietnamese militiamen."

Villagers were reluctant to use drums, flares, and smoke just to announce the presence of the Viet Cong, in case the act of just signaling provoked an attack. Smoke signals, when they were used, proved ambiguous, with the Viet Cong copying Allied signals to lure ARVN relief forces into ambushes and traps. It was clear that secure two-way radio communications were needed for the villages.

Civilian engineers working for the US Operations Mission, an aid agency of the State Department, came up with the solution.

Paul Katz, one of the engineers, was given the task of providing a radio set for police and paramilitary units. He found that US military radios were too heavy, complex, and expensive. Existing US police radios were unsatisfactory. Their operating range was too short for the 10-20-kilometer distances between villages in Vietnam. In April 1961 Paul Katz designed a simple portable radio that eventually became standard issue for the villages. It was an AM

voice set with 20 watts of power that Katz named the TR-20. Through State Department channels, he got a bid from a manufacturer to produce 2,000 sets in three months for police and paramilitary use.

Secretary McNamara's people learned about the project and recognized the military value of the TR-20. It could be used by villages to alert regular ARVN units to VC presence and actions. McNamara directed the US Army in February 1962 to help the TR-20 project.

Installation of the TR-20s in villages got under way in March 1962. The VC attempted to prevent the work, but it moved ahead rapidly. Advisers reported that arrival of the radio and inauguration of its use was a big ceremonial event. For the village chiefs it was the ultimate prestige item. Just keeping the TR-20 radios in their homes was felt to be an honor.

Next, McNamara wanted radios installed in the hamlets, which were subdivisions of villages, and the smallest unit of local government in Vietnam. But the TR-20's power and range was too much for the hamlets, so Katz designed smaller versions. Named for their wattage, they were the TR-5 and HT-1 (H is for hand-held).

These gadget radios were well suited to the requirements. By early 1963, more than 2,000 hamlets and villages had 2,613 of Katz's little radios and were linked with district and province capitals. Army Special Forces units ordered the sets for all of their camps. They were especially keen on the little HT-1. It operated off flashlight batteries, which were readily available, and had a range of 15 kilometers, greater than the range of the heavier military manpack radios issued by the Army.

Only one design flaw marred the HT-1 radio. Katz had incorporated a button on the set that had only one purpose. When pushed, it destroyed the entire circuit board, so the enemy could not use the radio if it was captured. But South Vietnamese irregulars either pushed it by mistake or as an excuse to abort a mission. So Paul Katz eliminated the self-destruct feature in later production versions.

When US Army ground combat units began arriving in Vietnam in mid-1965, they had modern tactical radios using solid-state circuitry. This was not due to unprecedented foresight about needing radios in Vietnam, but because the Army had been an early supporter of the development of mass-produced equipment using the transistor.

Roger that —An infantry officer uses a civilian hand-held walkie-talkie REC-6 radio during operations. Many sets like the REC-6 were tested by the Army in Vietnam, but few were adopted.

The standard infantry manpack radio of the day was the AN/PRC-25 (nicknamed "Prick 25"). An FM voice set, the PRC-25 was reliable, simple to use, and had a range of up to 15 kilometers in rough country. It netted with—that is, could talk with—the Army's whole family of vehicle and aircraft FM tactical radios. General Creighton Abrams, MACV deputy commander in 1967 and later Westmoreland's successor as commander, called the PRC-25 "the single most important tactical item in Vietnam."

PRC-25s were carried by RTOs (Radio-Telephone Operators) at platoon level and higher. The RTO is the young man so often seen in combat photos leaning slightly forward to offset the weight of his PRC-25 and combat gear, and with an antenna sticking high into the air above him.

No radios were issued below platoon level to rifle squads or machine gun teams. Because army planners expected to fight in Europe and not the jungle, communication between platoon leaders and their squad leaders was expected to be accomplished by yelling or hand signals. Squad leaders were expected to control their men the same way. Unfortunately, the troops were fighting in Vietnam, where dense jungle hid hand signals, and yelling gave away your position to the enemy, who might be only a few feet away.

A squad radio was needed. Such a radio had been under development for several years. Now, combat necessity accelerated its development. The radio consisted of two units, a transmitter (the PRT-4) and a separate receiver (PRR-9). The squad leader had both. Riflemen and other squad members would have only the receiver. The receivers, weighing only 8.6 ounces, were worn clipped to each man's helmet. Transmitters were hand-held and weighed 18 ounces.

The first 400 models arrived in Vietnam in March 1967. Technically they were satisfactory and met the specifications. But the troops did not like the radios and took little care of them. Mostly they disliked the one-way nature of the communication. The heat and humidity affected the batteries, turning them into soggy cardboard. The radio had no antenna and the grunt's steel helmet was meant to served double duty as both an antenna and protective headgear. The plan quickly broke down when in the steamy heat of the jungle men discarded their helmets and suffered a consequent loss in reception and put the blame on the radios. After a while the troops stopped trying to adjust their behavior to the radios, leaving the gadgets behind at fire bases when they went out on patrol. One observer noted that, "Many com-

manders consigned them to footlockers . . . where they remained for the rest of the war. An attempt to save money had led to the development of a rarely used two-section radio costing $1,044 each."

Balloons were tried as a means of extending the range of existing radios. In the Mekong Delta, the 9th Infantry Division's signal battalion had the problem of communicating longer than normal distances to units dispersed among the thousands of square miles of mangrove swamp and canals. They obtained a balloon and filled it with 4,000 cubic foot of helium. An FM transmitter was attached to the balloon, which was tethered and sent aloft. Radio range increased greatly. But the balloon had to be abandoned after high winds in the monsoon season knocked it down.

Resourcing radios for villages and squads was relatively simple compared to providing equipment

Command and control

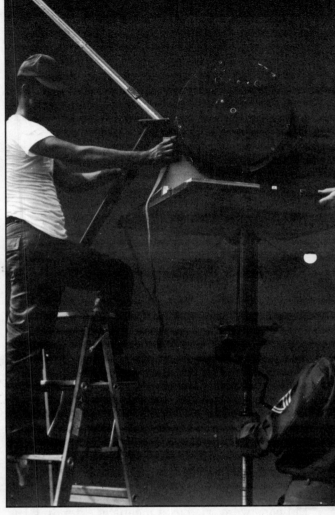

BEAM ME UP: Signalers erect a portable folding satellite dish at Tan Son Nhut airport in 1964 so that Washington could talk with Saigon in real time. Satellite communications were then still in their infancy and dishes needed to be large to pick up the comparatively weak signals coming from the low-powered satellite transmitters. As the power output from satellite transmitters power increased through improved solar cell arrays, so the size of dishes decreased.

for higher level communication. At battalion and brigade level, commanders required communications systems, not single radio sets. For commanders, radio was now an essential tool of war, of more importance than it had been in earlier wars.

This was partly because the fighting was more tightly controlled by Washington and intervening headquarters. The politicians and the higher commands demanded and got information from the fighting scenes in almost "real time." Television and radio broadcast newsmen were able to transmit their pictures back to the States to be broadcast within

24 hours. In the White House and Pentagon it was essential to know what was happening before it burst on the nation's living room screens.

The fluid nature of the combat in Vietnam meant that telephone lines could not be laid on the battle-field as had been done in the Korean War and the two world wars. Outside their base camps, fighting units flew by helicopter to the next scrape, or in-filtrated on foot. Trying to fight a battle from the traditional ground command post of earlier wars was out of the question. Radio was the medium of choice and of necessity.

Ready to talk —Sandals at the ready, an ARVN operator of a PRC-10 radio takes a break while awaiting airlift by US Army helicopters in February 1963. The RC-10 was temperamental and hard to calibrate. The PRC-25 backpack radio that succeeded it became the standard combat radio used by US and ARVN troops for the rest of the war.

Radio was essential to the concept of air mobility tested and validated by the 11th Air Assault Division from 1963 to 1965, with the tests leading to the formation of the 1st Air Cavalry Division in July 1965. Throughout the extensive tests, it was clear at all levels that commanders needed some sort of new radio console. A heliborne command post was needed to integrate the multiple radio sets that had to be used while flying to an action or during a fight.

Further adding to the requirement for airborne command consoles was the closer battlefield cooperation among the armed services. In Vietnam, Army and Air Force combat units operated together to degrees unprecedented in World War II and Korea. This was especially true for close air support and tactical airlift. In the northern provinces close to the DMZ, units of all four services routinely worked together.

Unfortunately in the years before Vietnam, technological cooperation had not preceded this interservice cooperation. Instead, each of the four services had developed their own equipment for their own special needs. Fighting units, aircraft, or ships had the radio gear they needed but could not necessarily talk to another service.

No one person better understood the price of this technological incompatibility than an infantry brigade commander aboard his command and control (C & C) combat assault Huey helicopter. With him aboard his C & C ship—known as a "Charley-Charley" to the grunts on the ground—was a sizable group. The pilot and copilot flew the aircraft and navigated. Often the pilot was the brigade aviation officer. Manning 7.62mm door guns on each side of the bird were the crew chief and a doorgunner. The brigade commander, either a colonel or a brigadier general, sat in the troop compartment, usually on the outside right seat on the same side as the pilot.

Also aboard the C & C ship in combat were the brigade operations or intelligence officer, the air liaison officer (a USAF fighter pilot detailed to duty with the brigade), and a senior artilleryman as fire support coordinator. Between them the command group used a wide array of radios that included:

- Two tactical FM command radios; one to talk with the infantry battalions making the com-

CHECKING IN:
A 1st Cavalry platoon leader keys the handset of his operator's PRC-25 radio to check with one of his squads. Sturdy and reliable, the PRC-25's effective range was 5 miles, making it ideal for field use.

bat assault or already in contact with the enemy, and another on the net of the next higher Army unit.

● One UHF radio for the air liaison officer to talk with close air support aircraft and forward air controllers.

● One tactical FM set for the fire support coordinator to talk with artillery fire direction centers or fire coordination centers.

● Up front with the pilots, one VHF and one UHF set for talking with transport helicopters and gunships.

●One HF single sideband set (optional) for long-range communications, particularly the air support operations net.

●Intercoms so that the commander and his team in the helicopter could converse with each other without transmitting over the radios.

●Frequency changers that allowed the commander to switch frequencies on the various radios as the situation required so that members of his command group could jump from one radio net to another.

●Scrambler devices to prevent the enemy eavesdropping.

Formal development work on the heliborne command post began with the air assault tests. Early versions were used in the skies over Vietnam by the 1st Cavalry Division in September and October 1965. Several improved versions were ready when the US buildup peaked in 1966-67. The rigs developed by the Signal Corps system had formal nomenclature, and were called AN/ASC-6, -10, -11, and -15. At the same time, enterprising communications officers in combat units built their own tailor-made communications consoles into their commanders' helicopters. But the end result was the same. The combat commander now had what he needed: He could control ground units, coordinate helicopter lift ships, fighter-bomber and gunship close air support, artillery fire support, and cope with emergencies.

Serving higher headquarters and flying at higher

altitudes over the war zone were the "talking birds," the Airborne Battlefield Command and Control (ABCC) aircraft. At the time they were the most sophisticated communications systems ever used in modern warfare. They were brought into action whenever several battles were happening over a wide swath of the war zone in South Vietnam or multiple strikes were being flown against North Vietnam and Laos. It was then that the air traffic burgeoned.

The air battle situation was unlike the everyday scenes on the radar screens of busy airports such as Heathrow, O'Hare, or JFK. At those fields the air traffic is aligned and mostly predictable with the aircraft at takeoff and landing speeds.

In the skies over Vietnam, aircraft of all sorts from all the services converged. They flashed past each other at cruise speeds or in afterburner. Over the North, with the additional hazards of enemy MiG fighters, surface-to-air missiles, and heavy flak, there was an even more critical command and control problem. The ABCC was devised to cope with it.

THE FUNCTIONS of command and control in Vietnam were helped by a cascade of developments in communications technology. Gadgets were created and sent to the war in record time, pushing the state of technology in the process. Commanders at all levels had better control over their forces and were

DROPPING THE WORD:

A bomb is loaded with leaflets to be dropped over an enemy-held zone. PSYOPS (psychological operations) teams improved upon the crude propaganda leaflet by developing new approaches. One of the most successful in persuading Viet Cong fighters to change sides was the "white envelope" concept, an idea using the hard-sell free gift technique of the direct mail shot. Each white envelope contained a letter appealing to the finder to put down his gun, a safe conduct pass, and a letter of amnesty from the local or district chief. Many were found by the Viet Cong or their families and many surrendered, clutching their safe conduct passes.

PSYOPS:
The wife of a Viet Cong guerrilla broadcasts an appeal to her husband in the bush. The microphone was hooked up to a radio transmitter that relayed her message to a bank of loudspeakers on a helicopter flying overhead.

able to react to enemy actions faster than their predecessors in World War II and Korea.

At the same time, the improved communications created problems that continue today and into the future. Senior commanders now had available the technology to enter a ground commander's radio net. Sometimes they could not resist the temptation to intervene in a situation, undermining the authority of the commander on the scene. Troops labeled such busybodies as "squad leaders in the sky." They orbited in C & C helicopters high above the blood, smoke, and noise of the fight, injecting unwanted advice into already crowded radio frequencies.

Less pernicious but more profound in its implications at all levels of command was the fact that as communications improved, the amount of information exploded. When new channels were created or existing ones improved, they were immediately loaded to capacity with more information. In his reflections on military communications in Vietnam, official historian John D. Bergen concluded that, "Parallel expansion not only offset the technical improvements in communications, but also increased the amount of data that had to be absorbed by commanders and their staffs. The Vietnam experience demonstrated that command and control do not necessarily improve as communications improve."

HEAR YE, HEAR YE:
A portable backpack loudspeaker system was a quick way to warn villages of an impending action against the VC. One unit prepared a booklet of 24 ready-to-broadcast messages in Vietnamese to cope with common situations. Another unit equipped its loudspeaker units with a cassette and player with messages in Vietnamese and the local ethnic tongue.

Bang on target

7

Advances in bomb technology

FROM THE START of combat aviation, fighter pilots have had to be intelligent and clever in order to survive. When they started shooting at each other, or at targets below, it was the pilots who provided the "smart" element while the airplanes and the bullets remained "dumb."

Such was the case through the development of combat aviation in World War II and the years leading up to Vietnam. It was also the case at the beginning of the Vietnam War with the ability of US fighter and attack aircraft to deliver bombs and bullets accurately on target solely determined by the brain, eyes, and motor skills of the man in the pilot's seat.

But by the end of the war, planes and weapons had become smart as well. And these revolutionary developments had as many implications for the future of modern warfare as did the appearance of the electronic battlefield.

Droploads early in the war were dumb bombs of various weights, such as the Mk 82 750-pound general purpose high explosive bomb. Pilots pointed their aircraft at the target and flew diving approaches at calculated airspeeds. At a certain specified altitude, they dropped the bombs and pulled up and away from the target.

As bitter experience and losses both showed, dumb bombs were invariably inadequate for the designated task. They did not pack enough power to destroy heavy targets like the Thanh Hoa bridge, a choke point on a strategically valuable highway leading to Hanoi. When they were used to bomb an area target, such as an airfield, they were not particularly accurate, although trained pilots could achieve impressive results. Often the only way to

115

The Bullpup weighed nearly 600 pounds, and carried a 250-pound warhead. Its maximum range was 7 miles, but for best guidance it had to be launched closer to the target. Each missile required a separate bombing run, and the standard load was two, giving twice the risk from flak, compared to ''dumb'' bombs.

increase the odds in favor of destroying a specific target was to saturate it with bombs carried by as many aircraft as could be made available.

The need to fly large numbers of aircraft over defended targets only served to increase aircraft losses. For the pilots of strike aircraft matters were made worse by adverse weather most of the year, long hours of flying, and an enemy who was constantly upgrading his air defenses. The 15,000 sorties a month flown by US strike aircraft in 1972 could only blunt, but not stop, Hanoi's offensive.

But even that ability to blunt the offensive of a determined enemy would not have happened without the advent of smart bombs.

The first early guided weapons, like the Bullpup (AGM-12) and Walleye (AGM-62) dated from the late fifties and early sixties. The Bullpup required radio guidance by the pilot, who could drop only one weapon per pass. The Walleye used television guidance.

Later US electronic warfare aircraft, known as ''Wild Weasels,'' used the radar-homing Shrike (AGM-45) for knocking out enemy surface-to-air missile (SAM) radars. But in a constantly escalating war of wits and technology, the radar operators at the SAM sites soon developed countermeasures

against the Shrike that diminished its effectiveness. Something better was needed.

This need was met by a new family of Electro-Optical Guided Bombs (EOGBs) and Laser-Guided Bombs (LGBs). Both types were heavy bombs, in the 2,000-3,000-pound range—a direct result of the failure of the frequent heavy poundings by conventional 1,000-pound bombs to destroy the strategically critical Thanh Hoa and Paul Doumer bridges.

The Electro-Optical Guided Bomb (EOGB) had a small television camera in the nose that showed where it was heading. A display scope in the back seat of the F-4E Phantom received the TV picture from the bomb. The pilot pointed the aircraft and bomb at the target. In the back seat, the Weapon Systems Operator found and designated the target for the EOGB. When the target was designated, the pilot released the EOGB and pulled away from the target, while the EOGB guided itself to the marked point on the target.

Darkness, clouds, smoke, and haze could limit the EOGB because its camera had to see the target clearly. But if conditions were right, the bomb went where it was aimed, while the airplane got away.

Laser-guided bombs used a laser seeker in the nose of the LGB that directed the bomb toward a target

TV GUIDED:

The nose of this AGM-62 Walleye guided bomb concealed a TV camera which transmitted a picture to the attack plane's Weapon Systems Operator. Once he had aligned cross wires on the target on his screen the 2,000-pound bomb was released and guided itself with its rear fins all the way to impact.

illuminated with laser energy by a laser emitter. The emitter could be on the same aircraft as the bomb, or on another aircraft. The LGB did not care where the energy came from. Regardless of the source of the laser energy it homed in on the laser-illuminated spot, known as the target aim point. Because of this, a single aircraft could serve as the laser illuminator for a strike by several other aircraft loaded with LGBs. As long as the laser energy struck the target continuously, the LGBs would direct themselves precisely there.

When the laser illuminator was on the same aircraft as the LGB, such as an F-4 Phantom, the Weapon Systems Officer (WSO) located the target aim point and illuminated it with the laser energy from a pod under the aircraft. The LGB would be linked with the target aim point. Then the pilot dropped the LGB and left the area. Even though he might be maneuvering the aircraft vigorously, as long as the WSO kept the laser beam striking the target, the LGB would hit it.

LGBs dropped from 20,000 feet had an 80 percent success rate in making direct hits. This, in turn, created savings in aircraft and bombs used. But like electronically guided bombs, laser-guided bombs required nearly clear atmospheric conditions. If clouds or fog or smoke broke the laser beam, the LGB reverted to being just another dumb bomb.

LGBs were first tested in combat over the Ho Chi Minh Trail during the long pause in bombing North Vietnam from November 1968 until the spring of 1972. In those tests, a forward air controller (FAC) flying an OV-10 Bronco aircraft provided the laser illumination on targets to be struck by F-4s carrying LGBs. The results showed how effective LGBs could be in destroying targets efficiently, and in reducing

SAM-KILLER: A Navy A-7E fires an AGM-45 Shrike antiradiation missile. The Shrike's homing head was turned on while the missile was still attached to the launch aircraft and fired as soon as the seeker head locked on to a target within its 16-mile range.

exposure to enemy air defenses. The first major test
of LGBs came in April 1972 after the North Vietnamese began their Easter Offensive and President
Nixon retaliated by ordering the resumption of air
strikes against North Vietnam.

The two key targets that had withstood hundreds
of air strikes in the bombing of the late 1960s were
the Thanh Hoa bridge and the equally bomb-
resistant, or so it seemed, Paul Doumer bridge.
(Senator Barry Goldwater calculated that by 1970
more than $28 million had been spent and many air-
craft lost trying to knock out the Thanh Hoa bridge.)

On 27 April 1972, F-4s unleashed five EOGBs
against the Thanh Hoa bridge through heavy flak
and poor visibility. The bridge was unusable to
traffic, but still stood. Then on 10 and 11 May 1972
in Hanoi, smart bombs finally managed to knock
down the main span of the Paul Doumer bridge. Two

Bang on target

SMART DROP:
Artist Keith Ferris' impression of USAF Thud 105s pulling away through the flak after one of the many attacks on the Paul Doumer bridge, Hanoi. After 177 sorties were flown against the mile-long rail-and-road bridge at a cost of two aircraft lost and fifteen damaged, smart bombs finally managed to destroy it in May 1972.

days later, on May 13, better weather provided the opportunity for another attack on the Thanh Hoa bridge.

Smart weapons made up the bulk of the bomb load that day. Twelve F-4s dropped eight 3,000-pound LGBs and sixteen 2,000-pound LGBs. Four more F-4s carried 48 Mk 82 general purpose bombs, to be dropped if bad weather prevented use of the smart bombs. Since the weather at the target was fine, both the smart and dumb bombs could be dropped precisely on target. When the smoke cleared, the once-indomitable bridge had dropped into the water.

THE USE OF LAND MINES was an area of technology where both sides in the Vietnam War showed ingenuity.

The VC planted mines on roads everywhere in South Vietnam. Before roads could be considered safe, mine detector teams had to sweep the roads and dig up the mines. In most populated areas where American troops operated, each day began with a patient sweep of the roads.

Where roads or trails were not swept, or where the sweepers failed to detect all the mines, casualties were heavy, with enemy mines and booby traps responsible for 20 percent of human casualties and 70 percent of US Army vehicle losses.

The enemy used mines based on Soviet and Chinese models with US forces unintentionally supplying large quantities of raw materials for both antitank and antipersonnel mines. Abandoned hand grenades, dud bombs, and other items of American ordnance were turned into deadly mines by the VC.

The newest of the US mines were known as Gravel mines—tiny devices developed by the US Army. They represented a new concept in minefields.

In previous wars minefields sown with antitank and antipersonnel mines had been seen exclusively as barriers to movement. Tactically they channeled the enemy along routes determined by the defending force. Mines had to be laid in precise patterns so that they could only be neutralized by digging them up and then individually disarming them. Otherwise an attacker blundering into a minefield risked being blown to bits.

Gravel mines did away with the need to dig precisely laid out minefields.

The XM-27 Gravel mine was so named because that is what it resembled—a chunk of gravel. Gravel mines were sown from the air onto trails or into areas where the enemy was concentrated or expected to enter. Looking like a gray and slightly aged teabag, they were small enough to lie hidden in the grass or the undergrowth, and powerful enough to blow off a man's foot. Because they had no metal casing they were impossible to detect with metal mine detectors.

The best feature of all, from the designers' point of view, was that Gravel mines were "self-sterilizing." Over a given period of time, usually a few weeks, they deteriorated and were no longer lethal. Gravel mines could be sown through an area to deny it to the enemy, who would quickly avoid the area once they had suffered their first few casualties. Then, after a predictable period of time

Deadly dish —This VC copy of a US Claymore antipersonnel mine packed 20 pounds of explosive and when detonated spewed rocks and steel fragments for 50 meters.

had elapsed, friendly troops could safely enter the area.

That was the design.

In field use, however, the self-sterilizing Gravel mines often failed to sterilize. US troops made that discovery the hard way, by losing feet in tramping through supposedly sterilized Gravel fields. MACV put it this way: "The first generation Gravel mine caused some anxiety, primarily because its self-neutralization system was unreliable and several unfortunate incidents occurred before the magnitude of the problem was fully realized."

"Magnitude of the problem" was bigger than those bland words suggest. It meant that no prudent commander would use them in an area where his troops might be expected to enter sometime in the future. Although the mines might actually have self-sterilized, it was impossible to be certain. The effect was that Gravel mines were not used in areas likely to be entered by US or ARVN troops.

However, Gravel mines were still handy for use in Laos and along the Ho Chi Minh Trail, and gave comfort to the defenders of Khe Sanh in the siege of 1968. According to MACV, more than a million were laid on the roads in nearby Laos and another million on the approaches leading into Khe Sanh.

Steady hands —An explosive ordnance disposal expert disarms a VC Claymore by pouring acetone through it, dissolving more than 20 pounds of TNT.

After the early poor results, scientists went back to the drawing board to improve Gravel mines. Before long they had three versions: the regular Gravel mine, one called Small Gravel, and a tiny MicroGravel. According to MACV, these improved versions could be expected to self-sterilize reliably, and even for a variety of time spans. However, commanders and troops remained skeptical of the self-sterilizing feature.

MicroGravel mines caused no damage, but they popped loudly when someone stepped on them. That set off acoustic sensors, giving warning of enemy movement.

"SPOOKY" is one of the most familiar nicknames from the Vietnam era. Like Dustoff, it also became part of the military lexicon. Spooky, now a generic term for fixed-wing gunships, was first applied to the AC-47.

The gunship concept was the result of fusing together a known aerial maneuver, the pylon turn,

Bang on target

PYLON TURN:
The basic principle of the fixed-wing gunship was the pylon turn whereby an aircraft circled about a target on the ground. Flying at approximately 4,000 feet and banking as it turned, a gunship allowed the gunners on board to hold a target steady in their sights. The gunship project was initially opposed by Tactical Air Command which feared that the gunships would prove too vulnerable to antiaircraft fire as they flew in a predictable circular pattern.

and a standard rapid-fire weapon, the 7.62mm minigun. In combination the two created a formidable new weapon system.

The pylon turn is a basic aerial maneuver. One of its most practical applications was devised by Nate Saint, a pilot missionary in South America, who was faced with the problem of delivering supplies and picking up mail from remote villages where his plane could not land. To solve the problem, Saint flew his light airplane in a pylon turn, describing a circle about a point on the ground below. At the same time he lowered a bucket on a long rope.

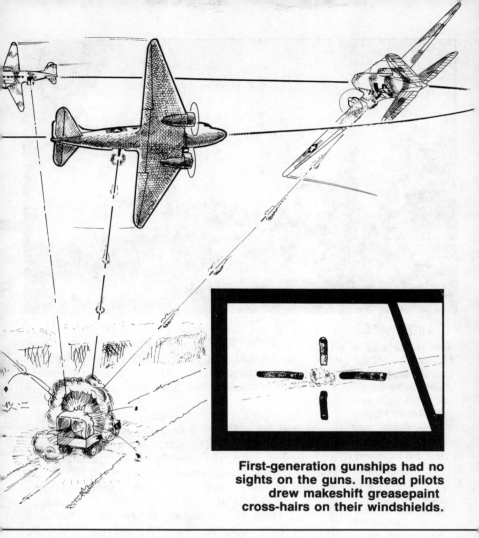

First-generation gunships had no sights on the guns. Instead pilots drew makeshift greasepaint cross-hairs on their windshields.

By flying the pylon turn properly, the bucket remained stationary at the point he desired. People on the ground took supplies from the stationary bucket and put outgoing items into it.

If the principle worked for a bucket on a rope, wouldn't it also be an effective way of shooting accurate aimed fire from an aircraft to a ground target? Getting from that question to the first AC-47 gunships took nearly two years of testing at Eglin Air Force Base, Florida, plus overcoming a lot of skepticism. But it worked.

In November 1964, General Curtis E. LeMay,

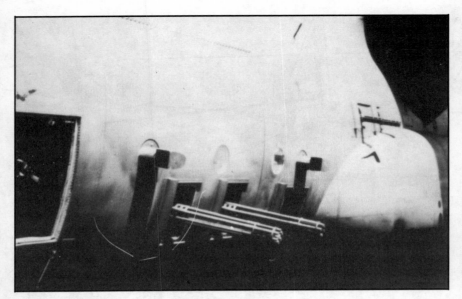

POTENT PUNCH:
The muzzle of a 105mm howitzer pokes out the port side of an AC-130 Spectre gunship. Fitted in 1972, the 105mm could fire a 44-pound shell over 7 miles, enabling it to stay out of the range of antiaircraft fire.

USAF Chief of Staff, ordered combat testing in Vietnam of modified C-47 Gooney Bird transports. Success was immediate. AC-47s broke up VC night attacks on outposts in several locations in December 1964 and January 1965. The rest, as they say, is history.

Through 1965 and into 1966, C-47s were rapidly converted into AC-47 gunships. AC-47s mounted three GAU-2/A 7.62mm multibarrel minigun pods, with plenty of ammo, flares, and crude gunsights for lateral firing. Nicknamed "Spooky" or "Puff the Magic Dragon," the gunships were on call almost every night, and usually had plenty of business.

Before long, the need for longer endurance and heavier firepower was clear. This led to Gunship II, the AC-130 Spectre, with four minigun pods and two 20mm cannon. The AC-130 went into action in December 1968 over Laos, but was beset by technical problems.

At the same time, however, modification of the C-119 Flying Boxcar into the AC-119G Shadow was under way. With a fourth gunpod and a searchlight, the Shadow went into combat over South Vietnam in January 1969. Next in the development chain was the AC-119K Stinger, which added two 20mm cannon and airborne sensors to the package. After technical problems, including being overweight,

12 Stingers were deployed to South Vietnam by December 1969.

In December 1970 a Stinger set a record for truck kills by a single AC-119 gunship in one night: 29 destroyed and six damaged along Route 92 in Laos. In February 1971, AC-119K Stingers were pitted against tanks as the NVA reacted to the South Vietnamese invasion of Laos on Operation Lam Son 719. In one night, 28 February, a Stinger destroyed eight PT-76 light tanks.

When the Tet Offensive of 1968 burst on the province capitals of South Vietnam, Spooky gunships helped blunt it.

My combat notebook for the night of 30-31 January 1968 carries this note, made at 0730 hours on the 31st: "Tam Ky (province capital) received mortar and ground attack at about 0530. Still in contact at 0730. No penetrations yet. Spooky and Firebirds on station, killing dinks in open."

When the attack began at 0530 hours, it was in total darkness with no moon or stars. The province chief called the 196th Light Infantry Brigade for help.

Because of the large number of refugees in Tam Ky and the unclear tactical situation, we did not want to use artillery. In turn, we called for Spooky and Firebirds (UH-1 gunships). They arrived within minutes, because the whole coastal area was on alert. We used Highway 1 running north-south as

THE FIRING SQUAD: Three 7.62mm miniguns aboard an AC-47 gunship. Each was capable of firing 6,000 rounds a minute. Gunships that combined miniguns, a 105mm howitzer, and electronic surveillance gear were the most feared of US aircraft.

Bang on target

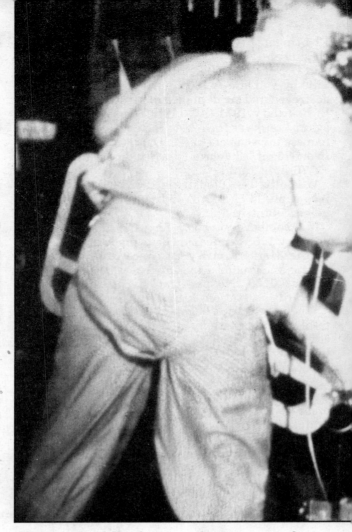

NIGHT DEATH:
Inside an AC-130 Spectre on a night mission, the crew loads and fires the big bird's 105mm howitzer at a target in the blackness below.

the fire control line between the two types of gunship. Spooky worked from Highway 1 eastward to the sea. Firebirds had responsibility from Highway 1 westward toward the jungled hills.

The light of their flares and searchlights showed up hundreds of enemy troops heading toward the province capital from all directions. The gunships went to work in a target-rich environment. Streams of red tracers gushed earthward from Spooky and the Firebirds, interspersed with the flash and crump of 2.75-inch rockets from the Firebirds. From the ground, muzzle flashes and green tracers showed the

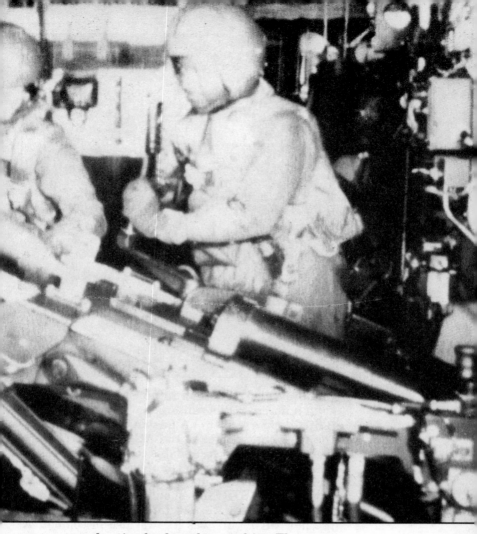

enemy was shooting back at the gunships. The province chief and his American advisers holed up at Tam Ky reported that the attackers had not broken into the town yet; the gunships were holding them off.

When the sun rose, we could see the state of the enemy. Some were stuck in the perimeter wire. Others lay dead or wounded outside the wire. Some of the survivors were shooting into the province capital compound, while others were fleeing westward. By 0800 hours the attack was over and the gunships flew home, with our thanks. The body

count revealed more than 250 enemy dead and more than a dozen POWs captured.

By the time of the NVA Easter Offensive of 1972, the teething troubles of the AC-130 Spectre were past. It was a most formidable combat weapon. But the enemy had been devising weapons of his own.

Friendly aircraft in 1972 had to face the new Soviet SA-7 STRELA shoulder-fired air-defense missile. Although western intelligence knew about the new SA-7, this was its first use in combat. A heat-seeker launched from a man's shoulder, the SA-7 was deadly in the Easter Offensive, bringing down several A-1, O-2, and OV-10 aircraft in April. (In June, an SA-7 also claimed the first kill of an AC-130 Spectre gunship southwest of Hue.)

Master Sergeant Arthur W. Humphrey, an illuminator operator on one of the AC-130 gunships, was among the first gunship crews to encounter SA-7 STRELAs. "Nobody in our squadron had even seen a STRELA. We had heard about them, but did not have much knowledge. We more or less learned by actually taking a hit." The first crewman to see a STRELA hit was in another aircraft on the night of 12 May. Humphrey said, "The guy who saw the first one, saw five of them at one time. He saw four, and the fifth one he didn't see."

The fifth SA-7 had homed in on a heat source on a searchlight, called a 2KW. The 2KW was in infrared (IR) mode at the time with its IR beam, invisible to the human eye, scanning the ground below to spot SAMs and flak, while its operator hung over the open tailgate of the C-130, held onto the airplane by a safety harness.

"We didn't know the STRELA would lock on the IR mode," said Sergeant Humphrey, "but it did. While the pilot was dodging the other four this one came up off his 9 o'clock position. When it locked onto the 2KW, it came in through that side (left-hand), and exploded inside the airplane, completely filling that side of the airplane with shrapnel. It hit the illuminator operator, caught him across part of his back and the back of his helmet. If he hadn't been in the down position, looking right underneath the

NIGHT SIGHT:
This infrared (IR) detector aboard an AC-119 Shadow gunship permitted the observer to view night scenes "illuminated" in infrared. The IR detector could "see" through the jungle canopy below to detect heat sources. The device was limited in scope and operators had to be trained to detect the difference between the heat radiated by truck engines and that generated by a herd of wild animals.

airplane, it probably would have taken off his head."

The illuminator operator survived, thanks to his helmet and flak vest. The pilot managed to fly the damaged aircraft back to Tan Son Nhut to make an emergency landing.

While the aerial bombs got smart and the fixed-wing gunships destroyed trucks, artillery ammunition also improved. Two projectiles are noteworthy because they were kept secret for so long, and were so devastating when unleashed. They were Beehive and COFRAM. They are based on the same concept, that of a single projectile carrying multiple rounds to a target.

Beehive warheads were created for howitzers, aerial rockets, and recoilless rifles. They were intended for close-in direct fire; that is, when the friendlies are almost eyeball to eyeball with the enemy. The basic principle was that the XM-546 Beehive projectile for the 105mm howitzer was packed tightly with 8,000 steel fléchettes, or arrows, each weighing 8 grains. The fléchettes constituted 9.14 pounds of the projectile's 38.25 pounds. (A Beehive round for the 106mm recoilless rifle carried 10,000 fléchettes.)

When the Beehive round was fired, the projectile casing ripped off early in flight, detonated by a time fuse. The fléchettes were ejected at high velocity in

STAGE LIGHTING: Inside an AC-119 Shadow gunship, a Fairchild technical representative (right) explains the operation of an illuminator control panel. The operator could choose flares, white light, or infrared illumination.

THE ULTIMATE TAKEOUT SERVICE

Gunship crews quickly built pride and a reputation for getting the job done under difficult circumstances. Many of them even had their own business cards.

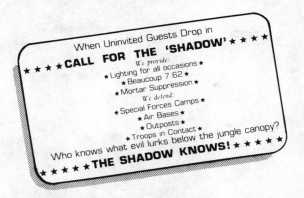

When Uninvited Guests Drop in
★ ★ ★ ★ CALL FOR THE 'SHADOW' ★ ★ ★ ★
We provide:
★ Lighting for all occasions ★
★ Beaucoup 7.62 ★
★ Mortar Suppression ★
We defend:
★ Special Forces Camps ★
★ Air Bases ★
★ Outposts ★
★ Troops in Contact ★
Who knows what evil lurks below the jungle canopy?
★ ★ ★ ★ THE SHADOW KNOWS! ★ ★ ★ ★

an expanding cone at about waist height. In flight, the 8,000 fléchettes buzzed like a swarm of bees; hence the nickname.

Beehive rounds were kept secret for some time and artillery units first received limited supplies late in 1966. They were a round of last resort. Beehive was fired when everything else had been shot at the enemy and he still kept coming.

In Operation Junction City during February and March 1967, Beehive was used to good purpose in hard-fought actions at Prek Klok and FSB Gold. US troops coming across enemy bodies on the battlefield described the dead VC as looking like pincushions—akin to the old drawings of Gulliver pricked by hundreds of Lilliputian arrows.

In late 1967, COFRAM (Controlled Fragmentation Munition) was even more secret than Beehive, which had been used many times by then. The code word could not be used with the full meaning, nor linked with artillery projectiles in unclassified usage. The sheer scale of the human carnage it could create made it a politically sensitive subject. To obtain authority to use COFRAM required clearance at the highest level with General Westmoreland, himself, approving the release of COFRAM rounds for use during the siege of Khe Sanh, during January-April 1968.

HELICOPTER BOMBER:

By stacking several dozen 81mm mortar rounds carefully in a tilted box with a trapdoor, the 173d Airborne Brigade made the UH-1D Huey into a mini-bomber. Over the target, the crewman opened the trapdoor and the rounds streamed out, exploding on impact below.

Whereas Beehive was used at close-in enemy troops, COFRAM rounds were fired over artillery distances ranging up to 18,000 meters by 155mm howitzers. The purpose was the same: to inflict heavy damage on large numbers of enemy troops. Inside each COFRAM projectile were 60 submu-

nitions, each a small grenade. Over the impact point, the projectile burst, scattering the submunitions over a wide area. They exploded on impact, scattering steel over a much wider area than conventional high explosive rounds.

Safety and comfort

Provision and requisition

THE GRUNT in the frontline welcomed any technical help he could get if it gave him an advantage over the enemy and made life marginally more tolerable in the steamy jungle heat of Vietnam. But no matter how slick the gadgets he was given, every American in the combat zone reserved his strongest concentration for the most important thing—going home alive. He welcomed any innovation that increased his chances for boarding the "Big Bird" back to the "World" when his tour was completed. At the same time, gadgets that made his stay in the war zone more comfortable were also cherished.

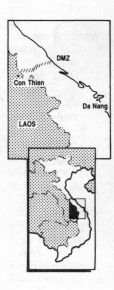

One scheme that helped was ENSURE, a program designed to leapfrog the normal development process. It stood for Expedited Nonstandard Urgent Request for Equipment. With the normal development process, years might pass between identifying a requirement and fielding of a gadget to meet it.

Under ENSURE, however, the process was shortened with lightning speed. A unit in the field with an urgent combat requirement stated it in simple terms, and suggested how it might be met. The unit's request was expedited to the Army back in the States to buy a commercial item that seemed to fill the combat requirement. Once bought, the item was shipped by air to the unit that had requested it, so that it could be tested.

In mid-1967, the 196th Light Infantry Brigade, then part of Task Force Oregon in the northern part of South Vietnam, used ENSURE to bring in much-needed equipment. A major responsibility of the 196th was the protection of Chu Lai air base and its dozens of Marine fighter-bomber aircraft. To keep

Totally neat —Paratroopers of 3/319 Artillery, 173d Airborne Brigade, with the tools to make the camp neat and remove the tall grass obstructing their line of vision —a lawn mower and scythe. Under the ENSURE program any commercially available item could be quickly obtained, with permission, if a combat unit could demonstrate an urgent need for it.

the enemy off balance and unable to launch rockets or mortars into the air base, infantry companies of the 196th operated far out into the bush.

But enemy action along Highway 1 and the rivers feeding into the sea above and below the Chu Lai base had complicated the task. Enemy sappers planted pressure-detonated and command-detonated land mines somewhere along Highway 1 every night. The pressure-detonated mines exploded when vehicles passed over them. They could be adjusted to let light vehicles and men pass without exploding, but blow up when a truck or tank drove over them.

Command-detonated mines were connected by wires to a generator concealed some distance away from the road. An operator would watch the road, wait for a vehicle to arrive over his mine, then crank the generator. Electricity would surge down the line to the detonator and the mine would explode beneath the target vehicle.

Before traffic could move each day, Highway 1 had to be swept for mines. Standard Army mine detectors were not as effective as they should have been. Also they were heavy and tiring to use. Stretches of road that had been shelled or had seen a lot of fighting carried thousands of minute pieces of metal. The standard detectors could miss land mines with relatively small metal content.

The 196th's Major Warren Lawson saw an advertisement in a Stateside magazine offering "treasure finders" for sale. These were metal detectors for use along beaches or old battlefields to find metal artifacts. Lawson recommended buying a batch of these devices under the ENSURE program. They would augment the authorized complement of Army-issue minesweepers, and could be more effective. General Frank H. Linnell, the brigade commander, endorsed the idea. Lawson sent in the request.

The treasure finder company soon responded. Lawson remembered, "They wrote us back, saying that they did not feel that their systems would be suitable for our use!" The order was reiterated, and the "treasure finders" soon flew in. They were quite useful, being much lighter and easier to operate than the issue minesweepers. They were cheap and plentiful and they worked.

Treasure finders helped, and the word was passed

Safety and comfort

LUMPY RICE:
A paratrooper of the 173d Airborne Brigade uses a PRS-3 metal detector to scan a sack of captured rice for hidden boobytraps. Since the standard Army issue detectors could miss land mines with relatively little metal content, the 173d used the ENSURE program to request and receive the type of commercial metal detectors popular with treasure hunters in the USA.

RIVERINE FORCE:
Men of the 196th Light Infantry wade along the banks of the Song An Tan, a river in I Corps Tactical Zone used as a supply route by the Viet Cong. The 196th, an infantry brigade with no boat experience, used five converted Boston Whalers fitted with outboard motors acquired under the ENSURE program to police the river.

to other units. But no amount of gadgetry could totally conquer the enemy's mine laying program throughout Vietnam for the duration of the war. Two years later, the 11th Armored Cavalry Regiment operating in the III Corps zone north and west of Saigon, encountered more than 1,100 mines in the year from June 1969 to June 1970. Sixty percent of them were detected and disarmed. The other 40 percent were only found when they blew up vehicles. In that single year, the 11th Cavalry lost 352 combat vehicles to mines. Its total authorized vehicle strength was less than 900. Countrywide, enemy land mines caused 73 percent of US tank losses, 77 percent of the M-113 armored personnel carriers lost, and 75 percent of all vehicles lost.

The 196th also used the ENSURE program to improve its patrolling of the An Tan river northwest of the base. The men of the 196th were sure that VC units used the river for moving supplies and men. But as an infantry brigade, the 196th was not authorized to have boats. Nonetheless it needed some to patrol the Song An Tan.

Patrick Dinapoli, one of the lieutenants in the 196th, was a boat enthusiast back in the States. He suggested using ENSURE to meet the need for boats. His commanding general agreed, and Dinapoli checked his boating magazines to decide on the right one. He chose an 18-foot Boston Whaler, powered by a 50 HP outboard motor. Once more the requirement was written, solution suggested, and sent off into the ENSURE system.

In less than two weeks, the brigade supply officer received a telephone call from the aerial port officer at the Chu Lai base. He wanted to check on a strange cargo just landed. A C-141 Starlifter transport had arrived from the States a few minutes before, carrying a priority cargo for the 196th. It was five light-blue Boston Whaler boats and several outboard motors in crates. Could that possibly be right? It was, and the load was soon in the hands of the 196th.

After covering the light blue with olive drab paint, the Boston Whalers were ready for duty on the Song An Tan. Volunteers were sought, and checked out on water operations. M-60 machine guns were mounted on the Whalers. Under command of the 2d Battalion, 1st Infantry, the boats went to work. One man took the helm, while a patrol of four or five men rode with him. The squads operated both night and day, sometimes using the motor, other times drifting or paddling for stealth. The immediate result was to throw the VC off balance, depriving them of the unfettered use of a waterway they had once considered their private highway.

FOOD WAS NEVER FAR from the thoughts of the average grunt. Tasty and nourishing food brightens a soldier's day and bad food ruins it. At the large permanent bases in Vietnam, troops ate hot meals three times a day. On the forward fire bases, hot meals with fresh food were served once or twice daily. Grunts on the ground in the jungle subsisted on combat rations, the C-ration.

For them hot meals were few and far between. Depending on the situation and unit policy, a hot meal in insulated containers might be served to rifle companies in the bush at noontime every fourth or fifth day. That was when resupply choppers flew in. They brought ammunition, replacement troops, mail, and more C-rations.

Some commanders thought that troop morale would be higher if they flew a hot lunch out to the forward units every day. It sounded good, but was a dumb policy. If enemy troops were nearby,

High Tech Detector —A military policeman uses a mirror on an angled shaft to scan the underside of a vehicle for contraband. The device was rough-and-ready and ineffective in the hands of bored or lazy troops.

INTO THE TREES

THE JUNGLE TREETOP LANDING NET was a novel solution to the recurring problem of how to quickly get men into areas where the jungle canopy was so dense that even a rope ladder could not be guaranteed to reach the ground.

The rig was made of flexible steel cabling connected by rigid rods. It was flown to the treetop landing site coiled under a UH-1D Huey helicopter. At the chosen clump of trees, the rig was untied and stretched below the Huey. As the helicopter

pilot flew slowly forward, the landing net snagged the treetops, forming a stable but flexible platform, safe enough for men to jump from the helicopter onto it.

However, once on top of the trees, the soldiers had a problem—how to get down. Primary jungle canopy could reach 100-150 feet or more above the ground. Secondary growth was somewhat lower, but more entangled and interwoven.

In reality, the men were marooned on top of the jungle. The rig was not used widely for that reason, but found occasional use as a means of setting up a clandestine observation post.

Home comforts —Ammo boxes were the raw material used to construct this shaving stand at the 196th Light Infantry Brigade's command post.

helicopters fluttering in gave away the friendly unit's precise location. That was a setup for a night mortaring or attack. The more prudent policy—one that saved lives—was to leave the fighting units alone so the company commanders and platoon leaders could move their men stealthily in an assigned area.

This meant that the grunts out in the field mostly ate C-rations. One C-ration was food for one soldier for one day. A C-ration was a 5-inch square cardboard box holding a variety of cans and packages and weighing just over 2 pounds.

Main dishes—if they could be called that—were canned. Among them were sausage patties in congealed white fat, beans and franks, and spaghetti and meatballs. In their favor it could be said that they were filling and nourishing, providing close to 3,000 calories per day, adequate for a campaigning trooper.

They had their drawbacks. C-ration meals were not very tasty. They tasted better when heated. But often that was impossible. Variety came with sticky cheese paste and bland crackers. Fruit cake and cookies from the Mother Cookie Co. made up the pastry part of many meal boxes. The real treat was getting a C-ration that included canned fruit as dessert. That made your day. Since C-rations came 12 to a carton and each individual ration was coded, astute soldiers quickly memorized the code numbers for the C-rations containing canned fruit and made sure they snaffled them first.

An essential gadget for eating C-rations was the all-purpose can opener nicknamed the P-38. Every man carried his own P-38, hanging off his dogtags or stashed somewhere on his gear. Inside each case of 12 Cs were three or four P-38s, just in case someone lost his.

Weight and bulk were the other major strikes against C-rations. Carrying enough C-rations for four or five days of operations added 10 pounds of weight, lots of sharp corners, and bulk that no fighting soldier took by choice. The cans and boxes created a garbage problem and potential hazard. (One of the VC's most innovative booby traps used a discarded C-ration can as the casing.)

Fortunately the Army had been working on improvements before the big troop buildup in Vietnam.

Safety and comfort

GOOD CHILI:
Out in the bush, a member of a long-range patrol digs into his freeze-dried chili. Lurp rations, named after the Long Range Reconnaissance Patrols, or LRRPS, were considered a real improvement on C-rations.

145

Canned food —An officer waits to board a troop transporter. The bulky C-ration box under his arm held canned food for 12 men for one day, and weighed more than 25 pounds.

The war accelerated the work, resulting in one of the most welcomed innovations, the Lurp ration, named after the Long Range Reconnaissance Patrols, or LRRPs, for whom it was intended.

Lurp rations benefited from the application of the freeze-dried process to combat rations. In freeze-drying, food is taken suddenly from room temperature to super-cold. At the same time, all liquid is extracted. The dried food is sealed in vacuum packs and returned to room temperature. In that state, the food has a long storage life, measured in years, and retains its flavor and fresh taste. Weight is also saved. Two-thirds of the weight of a canned C-ration was water. When freeze-dried, two-thirds of the weight disappeared.

Better yet from the grunts' viewpoint was how tasty the Lurp rations became. The chili meal was especially zesty. Ice cream (freeze-dried), banana flakes, and other delicacies were in the vacuum pouches. Unlike C-ration cans that cut and gouged a man, Lurp ration pouches were malleable, bending and tucking away anywhere a man had space.

Preparation of Lurp rations was easy. All a grunt needed was potable water to add to the package. It was then stirred or kneaded and allowed to stand for a few minutes for the water to be absorbed. The meals tasted good, either hot or cold.

First issued to LRRPs and other special units, the Lurp rations were an immediate success. Word quickly spread and demand from the troops led to their widespread issue to other combat units. C-rations remained in the system, but the tasters' choice was clearly in favor of the Lurp ration.

Good food was a primary need of every grunt. Another need was to survive. His thoughts always acknowledged the possibility of being hit. His steel helmet gave some protection to his skull. With the entrenching tool, he could—and did—dig into the ground to find protection from enemy fires.

But for walking around, he needed flexible protection. That was provided by the armored vest, popularly called the flak vest or flak jacket. Made of multiple interwoven layers of flexible synthetic materials under a tough, dark, nylon outer coat, the flak jacket weighed about 12 pounds. It was actually an oversize vest that could be worn over other clothing.

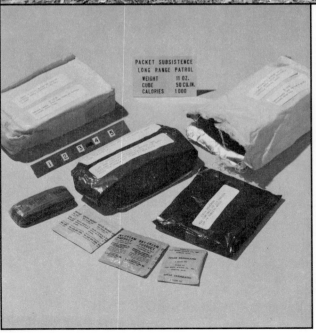

PACKET SUBSISTENCE
LONG RANGE PATROL
WEIGHT   11 OZ.
CUBE   50 CU.IN.
CALORIES   1 000

CHOW DOWN:
Troops in the field enjoy a canned meal of C-rations. The cans added weight and provided useful material for an enemy constantly foraging for materials to make mine and grenade casings. The Lurp ration (below) had only one-third the weight of a C-ration and tasted better.

To satisfy the grunts' needs to carry everything, pockets abounded on the flak jacket. Its function was to protect the body's most vital organs, and it worked. Flak jackets gave a high measure of protection reaching from the neck down to below the waist. This gave protection to heart, lungs, liver, kidneys, stomach, spleen, and most of the intestines. Most grunts appreciated the protection without being told. The few who scoffed at wearing flak jackets usually changed their minds after seeing dead men for the first time.

The value of the flak jacket was underlined by casualty data from the 1st Battalion, 6th Infantry (1/6) during a hard fight against NVA troops during fighting around Da Nang in February 1968. Lieutenant Colonel William J. Baxley, 1/6's commander, had stressed to his men the need to wear flak jackets and steel helmets. In one day of exceptionally tough fighting, Baxley's outfit lost 15 men killed and 55 wounded. Because his men wore their flak jackets, only 17 percent of the wounds they suffered were to the torso and head even though those parts constitute more than 40 percent of the surface area of the human body. This low injury rate to the head and torso was directly attributable to wearing flak jackets and steel helmets.

FLAK JACKET: A helicopter crew chief dons his flak jacket before a mission. Surveys showed that flak jackets, which incorporated a thin layer of steel mesh, helped to reduce injury rates.

In mechanized and cavalry units, men tried to own two flak jackets. Riding along in an M-113 armored personnel carrier, they wore one jacket. They sat on the other, to protect the vital family jewels.

North Vietnamese troops also had flak jackets. US Marines fighting NVA units around Con Thien south of the DMZ in May 1967 observed them wearing flak jackets and steel helmets.

Another gadget grunts considered essential for survival in the field was the Claymore mine. It was developed by the Army before Vietnam, and was soon an essential item in everyone's kit. The name came from the large, double-edged Scottish broadsword.

Weighing only 3.5 pounds, in action the Claymore was a crowd-killer. It was an antipersonnel mine that shot a deadly fan of steel projectiles from ground level to waist high, and out to 50 meters.

To place a Claymore required only unfolding the short legs and sticking them into the ground,

BIG ZIPPO:
An M-132 "Zippo" flamethrower fires a burst of napalm to flush out Viet Cong snipers in a bunker. Troops nicknamed the carrier "Zippo" after the dependable and rugged cigarette lighter made by the Zippo Co. of Bradford, Pennsylvania.

Smart woodwork —A staircase constructed from parts of 155mm ammunition boxes improved the footing at Charger Hill, base for a time for the 196th Light Infantry Brigade. Improvisation was a constant challenge and need. There were few other creative outlets in the combat zone.

making sure that the front was aimed toward the enemy. When detonated, the fan of projectiles exploded in that direction only.

The Claymore was command-detonated. It was used most often in defensive positions, where its ease of emplacement and deadly effect added to security. Wires led from the Claymore back to a listening post or outpost or bunker. When enemy troops entered the killing zone, a grunt squeezed the firing device and the mine exploded.

It was frequently used for ambushes as detonating the Claymore did not reveal the location of the ambushers. In the Ia Drang Valley fighting of November 1965, the 1st Battalion, 9th Cavalry (1/9) set up an ambush along a trail that an NVA regiment seemed likely to use. Eventually, a heavily laden NVA company came trudging along the trail soon after dark. The NVA troops then took a 90-minute break just outside the Claymore killing zone. The 1/9 Cavalry troopers waited silently. At 2100 hours, the enemy saddled up and began tramping along the trail right into the killing zone. The 1/9 Cavalry had placed eight Claymores to command a 100-yard stretch of trail. When the enemy weapons platoon was strung along the Claymore line, the trap was sprung. The NVA platoon was wiped out.

GADGETS NEITHER WON nor lost the war in Vietnam. The NVA and VC benefited from technology, too, and applied ingenuity to tactical problems just as US forces did. In 1972 the air defenses of Hanoi were probably among the best in the world.

But the most profound effect came from the US effort to provide US forces with the fruits of modern technology—in the process often helping to advance the technologies themselves.

The process laid the foundation for future developments, many of which are now considered commonplace. Hovercraft now provide a regular cross-Channel service between Britain and France. Satellite communications bring the world into the living room in real time. Intrusion devices are standard components for industrial and residential security.

General William C. Westmoreland, who com-

Safety and comfort

BLOW 'EM AWAY:

The M-18A1 Claymore antipersonnel mine was at the heart of the concept of the "mechanical ambush." Packed with steel pellets Claymores were sure killers out to 30 meters, and frequently wounded people at ranges of 40 meters or more. Once the Claymore's steel legs had been unfolded an operator used the sight on top to aim the Claymore. The mine was armed with a blasting cap connected by 50 feet of wire to a hand-held firing device that used two flashlight batteries. When the handle on the device was depressed, the Claymore fired.

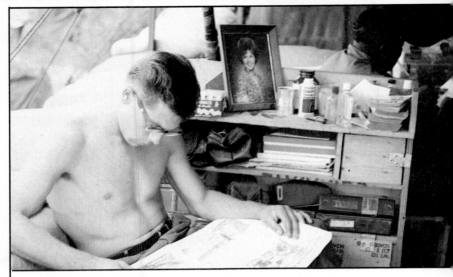

AMMO BOXES, FOR THE USE OF:

GRUNTS CREATED their own homemade gadgets for comfort and safety in the combat zone. The most common source of materials was the ordinary wooden ammunition box. In any combat area, they proliferated and were available for the asking. Ammo boxes were turned into all sorts of furniture, including shower stalls, armchairs, shaving stands—even altars by padres in the field.

Standard military issue ammo boxes were a do-it-yourselfer's dream come true. The boxes, made of 37 different types of wood (all at least 11/16" thick), were held together with heavy nails and fitted with metal hasps and hinges, and rope handles for lifting. They conformed to military specifications (MilSpec B-2427E) and were built to take rough knocks in transit so that the mortar and artillery rounds they contained arrived at the guns ready to shoot.

manded US forces in Vietnam during the most intense application of gadgets to fighting the war, and later became the Army's Chief of Staff, clearly believed that the changes he had presided over would influence future wars. He has predicted that, "On the battlefield of the future, enemy forces will be located, tracked, and targeted almost instantaneously through the use of data links, computer assisted intelligence evaluation, and automated fire control. . . . I am confident the American people expect this country to take full advantage of its technology—to welcome and applaud the developments that will replace wherever possible the man with the machine."

This is the "electronic battlefield," the remote con-

trol war where gadgets are surrogates for men. The Defense Department continues strong efforts in that direction. Consider the names of a few projects DoD supports for research out to 1991: Joint infrared laser/seeker, automatic target recognition for smart weapons, guided tactical hypervelocity missiles, multisensor autoprocessors, liquid propellant guns, and more.

Those projects sound exciting and powerful. But future national leaders will be well advised to remember that gadgets will not necessarily win wars. The other side has gadgets, too. Gadgets are important and helpful, but wise and resolute national leaders are worth more.

AAA	— Antiaircraft artillery.
AAM	— Air-to-Air Missile.
ACTIV	— Army Concept Team for Vietnam.
ACV	— Air cushion vehicle.
ACOUSID	— Acoustic and seismic intrusion device.
ADSID	— Air dropped seismic intrusion device.
Agent Orange	— Herbicide used for defoliation.
AGM	— Air-to-Ground Missile.
AGM-45	— Shrike air-to-ground missile, antiradiation type.
AGM-78	— Standard Arm air-to-ground missile, antiradiation type.
AIM	— Air-intercept missile.
APC	— Armored personnel carrier, usually M-113.
ARC LIGHT	— B-52 operations in Southeast Asia.
ARVN	— Army of Vietnam (South).
Beehive	— Artillery projectile that spews 8,000 steel fléchettes.
CA	— Combat assault by helicopter.
C & C ship	— Command and control helicopter.
CBU	— Cluster Bomb Unit.
Charlie	— Nickname for the Viet Cong, stemming from the phonetic alphabet call sign "Victor Charlie."
CINCPAC	— Commander-in-Chief Pacific.
Claymore	— US command-detonated anti-personnel mine used in perimeter defense and ambush. Throws a large number of oval steel pellets in a fan-shaped blast.
Commando Hunt	— Operation in Laos to stop traffic on the Ho Chi Minh Trail.
Concertina	— Coiled barbed wire used in defensive positions.
CP	— Command post.
Crusher	— LeTourneau tree crusher, transphibian.
CS	— Riot control tear gas.
CTZ	— Corps Tactical Zone. South Viet-

Glossary

nam was divided into four CTZs, with I CTZ in the far north and IV in the Delta in the southernmost part of the country.

DCPG — Defense Communications Planning Group—the government agency that oversaw development of unattended sensors.

Defoliation — Use of chemicals such as Agent Orange to kill foliage.

DMZ — Demilitarized Zone.

Dustoff — Helicopter extraction, usually medical—also the radio call sign of medevac helicopters.

ECM — Electronic Counter Measures.

ENSURE — Expedited Nonstandard Urgent Request for Equipment.

EOGB — Electro-Optical Guided Bomb. One of the first "smart" bombs.

EW — Electronic warfare.

FAE — Fuel-air explosive, usually used in a CBU-55 cluster bomb.

Flak — Antiaircraft shrapnel fragments.

Field of fire — Area that a weapon or group of weapons may cover effectively from a given position.

Firefly — UH-1 Huey helicopter with high-intensity lights.

FO — Forward observer—artilleryman operating in the frontline.

FSB — Fire Support Base—defended perimeter containing supporting artillery and mortar units.

GCA — Ground Controlled Approach.

GCI — Ground Control Intercept.

Gravel Mine — Miniature antipersonnel land mine.

Greenseed — New arrival.

Gunship — Armed helicopter; UH-1 first, later the AH-1 Cobra.

HE — High Explosive.

Huey — UH-1 utility helicopter.

Igloo White — Code name for program for surveillance of NVA infiltration along the Ho Chi Minh Trail.

ISC	— Infiltration Surveillance Center for Igloo White.
JCS	— Joint Chiefs of Staff.
Jungle penetrator	— Device for lifting a man from dense jungle.
Killer Junior	— Direct defensive fires by 105mm and 155mm guns.
LAPES	— Low altitude parachute extraction system used with C-130 Hercules.
Laser	— Device that projects laser energy onto target designator.
LAW	— M-72 Light Antitank Weapon (66mm) with shaped charge, frequently used to demolish enemy fortifications.
LGB	— Laser Guided Bomb—a smart bomb.
LRRP	— Long range reconnaissance patrol, "Lurp."
LZ	— Landing zone; an area suitable for landing by helicopter.
M-16	— Rifle, 5.56 mm; individual weapon, capable of semi-automatic and automatic fire.
M-60	— Machine gun, 7.62 mm; standard infantry automatic weapon.
M-79	— Grenade launcher that fires 40mm shells out to 400 meters.
M-113	— Armored personnel carrier.
MACV	— Military Assistance Command Vietnam.
McNamara Fence	— Electronic barrier planned across the DMZ.
Mighty Mite	— M-106 dispenser commonly used to spread CS tear gas.
Nighthawk	— UH-1 helicopter modified for night missions.
NVA	— North Vietnamese Army.
Pave Eagle	— Beechcraft Debonair airplane used for radio relay.
People sniffer	— Device to detect micro particles in the air.
PPS-4	— Ground-based radar with range of 1.5 kilometers.

Glossary

PPS-5	— Ground-based radar with range of 5 kilometers.
Province	— Political subdivision of Vietnam comparable to a state within the US.
PSID	— Patrol seismic intrusion device.
Ranch Hand	— Operation flown by C-123 spray aircraft for defoliation.
Rome Plow	— D-7E or HD-16 bulldozer with Rome Plow blade for clearing jungle.
RPG	— Rocket propelled grenade— enemy grenade with shaped charge.
SA-2	— Soviet-built surface-to-air missile system.
SA-7	— STRELA hand-held heat-seeking SAM.
SAM	— Surface-to-air missile.
Shadow	— Nickname for AC-119G gunship.
Shrike	— AGM-45 air-to-ground radar-seeking missile.
Spectre	— AC-130 gunship (Gunship II), or Spooky AC-47 gunship, or C-47 transport converted to a gunship.
Starlight scope	— Passive night vision device (AN/PVS-2) that intensified available light.
Stinger	— Nickname for AC-119K gunship.
Tet	— Vietnamese lunar New Year.
Thud	— Nickname for the Republic F-105 Thunderchief.
TOC	— Tactical operations center.
VC	— Viet Cong.
Walleye	— Nickname for the AGM-62 air-to-ground missile, antimaterial type.
Wild Weasel	— F-100F or F-105F aircraft armed with radar homing and warning systems and antiradiation missiles. They could home in on SA-2 radar guidance signals to destroy the missile sites.
Zippo	— M-132 armored personnel carrier equipped with flamethrower.

About the Author

F. Clifton Berry, Jr.

F. CLIFTON BERRY, JR., was a paratrooper and airborne infantry officer in the 82d Airborne Division. He saw Vietnam combat as operations officer of the 196th Light Infantry Brigade, logging 600 flying hours in helicopters and FAC aircraft.

In an Army career, he commanded airborne and infantry units from squad through battalion level in the US and Far East.

Following active service, since 1975 he has been an editor and writer on military and aerospace topics. He was co-editor of *Armed Forces Journal*, editor in chief of *AIR FORCE Magazine*, and chief US editor of the Interavia publishing group. He is the author of *Sky Soldiers*, *Strike Aircraft*, and *Chargers*, companion volumes in the Illustrated History of the Vietnam War series.

He is a master parachutist and active pilot, with land and seaplane ratings.

THE ILLUSTRATED HISTORY OF THE VIETNAM WAR

ntam's Illustrated History of the
etnam War is a unique and new
ries of books exploring in depth the
r that seared America to the core:
var that cost 58,186 American lives,
at saw great heroism and re-
urcefulness mixed with terrible
struction and tragedy.

he Illustrated History of the
etnam War examines exactly what
ppened. Every significant aspect—
e physical details, the operations,

and the strategies behind them—is
analyzed in short, crisply written
original books by established
historians and journalists.

Some books are devoted to key
battles and campaigns, others unfold
the stories of elite groups and fighting
units, while others focus on the role
of specific weapons and tactics.

Each volume is totally original and
is richly illustrated with photographs,
line drawings, and maps.